30 Kayaking Tours within One Hour of Washington, D.C.

30 Kayaking Tours
within One Hour of Washington, D.C.

Steven Smolinski

First Edition

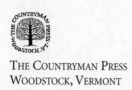

THE COUNTRYMAN PRESS
WOODSTOCK, VERMONT

Interior photographs by the author unless otherwise specified
Maps by Erin Greb Cartography, © The Countryman Press
Book design by Faith Hague
Book composition by PerfecType, Nashville, TN

Published by The Countryman Press, P.O. Box 748, Woodstock, VT 05091

Distributed by W. W. Norton & Company, Inc., 500 Fifth Avenue,
New York, NY 10110

Printed in the United States of America

10 9 8 7 6 5 4 3 2 1

30 Kayaking Tours within One Hour of Washington, D.C.
978-1-58157-159-2

To my beautiful wife, Karen, and our awesome parents,
Joe & JoAnn and Bill & Bamby

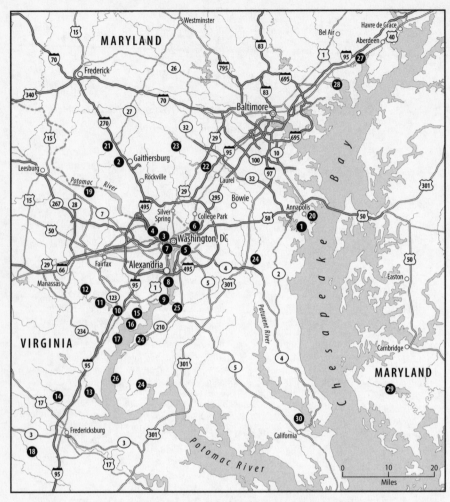

Numbers in black circles refer to sites listed in the Contents, opposite

Contents

Introduction

M Y WIFE, Karen, and I have been avid kayakers in the local Washington, D.C., area for over 10 years, and while there is a wealth of information on the Internet about places to paddle in proximity to downtown District of Columbia, there is no one single reference guide that includes a detailed description of numerous trips within an hour of the nation's capital. Being both busy professionals, we found it advantageous to limit the driving we have to do to pursue a particular recreational activity. While most of these routes cover a range of paddling times from, on average, 2 to 4 hours, almost all can be extended several more hours if desired.

We have paddled every one of these trips multiple times and in different seasons. We have found that shortly after dawn and just before the sun sets are the best times of day to view wildlife in these places. This is especially true during the peak season for water activities in the mid-Atlantic states, April to September. However, we have made several trips in the middle of the day and have often seen a wide variety of birds and aquatic wildlife.

Easy-to-follow directions to all put-in sites have been included for each trip, as well as information on facilities and other activities available at each location. Each trip has route descriptions and GPS waypoints to help guide you. Also, where applicable, we have provided historical notes of interest about the sites.

Finally, if you plan to paddle several of the sites in Northern Virginia, you should consider purchasing an Occoquan Watertrail League (OWL) pass for the year. The membership gives you year-round access to many of the parks and routes in this book, including Fountainhead, Occoquan Regional Park, Pohick Bay, Bull Run Marina (restricted

The author and his wife paddling the James River

access; additional $15 for a key), and Algonkian Park. The passes can be purchased at Fountainhead Regional Park, (703-250-9124), described in more detail in chapter 11. You can upload the OWL brochure at www.nvrpa.org/uploads/Files/content/OWLbrochuretake1.pdf.

Kayak Rentals

For those readers who do not have their own kayaks, or if friends join you who do not have kayaks, launch sites that rent them are listed below. Information about rental costs and amenities is included in each chapter.

Beginner Paddling Routes
1. Quiet Waters Park
2. Seneca Creek Park

Washington, D.C.
3. Thompson Boat Center
4. Fletcher's Boat House
6. Bladensburg Waterfront Park

The Four Seasons

Kayaking is a sport that can be enjoyed year-round in the mid-Atlantic states with the proper gear and preparation. We have paddled in every month of the year and have found different joys in each of the four seasons. Some of the most unique paddles have involved breaking through a thin layer of ice in some of the smaller channels at Columbia Island Marina in Arlington, Virginia, and Queen Anne Bridge on the Patuxent River in Maryland.

Tides and Winds

For those trips described here on waterways (as opposed to lakes or reservoirs), it's always best to check the tides, because, in many cases, accessibility in some of the smaller tributaries is restrained by water level. Also, while the tidal range in Virginia and Maryland tributaries averages only 1½ to 3 feet, when combined with a moderate breeze, this is enough to produce conditions that can challenge the fittest of paddlers. Paddling during slack-tide time (two hours before and after high and low tides) minimizes the effect of current associated with tidal fluctuations.

It is recommended you take a few moments before launch to assess the prevailing conditions, and if you have a choice (which most of these tours provide), it is usually best to paddle up-wind, against the current, first, so you will be less fatigued toward the end of the paddle. Sometimes winds can be very finicky, but you can usually ascertain a prevailing direction.

Please refer to the appendix, which lists Web sites that provide daily information on tides. With a few clicks of a mouse, you can find the current day's and next day's tides for sites up and down the Chesapeake Bay, Potomac River, and tributaries in Maryland and Virginia.

Recommended Gear

A properly outfitted kayaker and boat can make the difference between an enjoyable experience and one that you never wish to repeat. While this list is mostly common sense and by no means comprehensive, it suggests the basic gear necessary for a safe and enjoyable paddle.

Necessary

Along with drinking water, carry the following safety equipment, stored in waterproof bags:

Cell phone
First-aid kit
Flashlight
Paddle float
Sponge
Whistle

Recommended

Chart
Compass
Energy bars
Gloves (to avoid blisters)
Bilge pump
Polypropylene clothing (because it dries quickly)
Sunglasses (to fight reflection from water surface)
Sunscreen

Colder Weather

Booties
Lip balm
Dry clothing (tops and bottoms, stored in waterproof bags)
Spray skirt
Waterproof gloves

Nice to Have

Binoculars
Digital camera
GPS

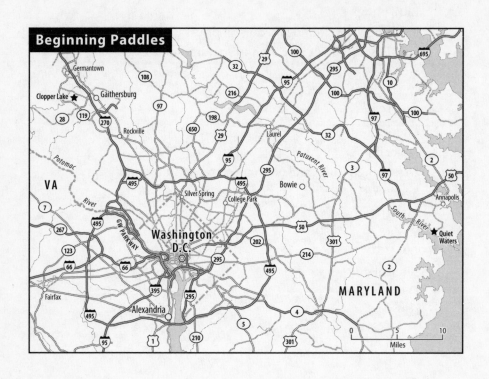

Beginner Paddling Routes

THE TWO PADDLING routes described here are ideal for the novice paddler for a few reasons. First, they are in relatively smaller, more sheltered bodies of water, thus providing greater protection from wind and wave effects; second, these sites rent kayaks; and third, paddling lessons are available as well.

If you have never paddled a kayak before, you should consider taking an introductory lesson or two to learn different paddling techniques, the various particulars of how kayaks handle, and, probably most importantly, how to be safe on the water.

In addition to the two sites described here, Lake Accotink in Northern Virginia is a good entry-level paddling route. This small (fifty-five-acre), shallow lake has a few islands to paddle around, a narrow creek to explore, and a very straightforward launch site. (Note that though they do not rent kayaks, they do rent canoes, rowboats, and pedal boats.) The park also has hiking and biking trails and basketball and sand volleyball courts. More information about the park can be found at www.fairfaxcounty.gov/parks/accotink.

1.

Harness Creek/South River: Quiet Waters Park

Directions: From I-495 (beltway), take exit 19, US 50, east toward Annapolis. Take exit 22, MD 665 (Aris T. Allen Boulevard), and stay on MD 665 until it ends and becomes Forest Drive. Follow Forest Drive for 2 miles. Turn right at the Exxon station onto Hillsmere Drive. (There is a sign in front of Exxon: QUIET WATERS PARK NEXT RIGHT.) The park entrance is 100 yards on the right-hand side. Entrance fee is $6, waived if you have a military ID. The park is closed on Tuesdays.

GPS Coordinates: 38° 56' 11" N; 76° 30' 34" W

Amenities: The 340-acre Quiet Waters Park has a wide variety of recreational activities in addition to kayaking, including 6 miles of paved hiking/bicycling trails that wind through forests and fields, a multilevel children's playground, tennis courts, and a South River Promenade and scenic overlook. The park is open 7 AM to dusk, and the visitors center, which includes a café, flower gardens, an art gallery, and public restrooms, is open Mon.– Fri., 9 AM–4 PM; Sat.–Sun., 10 AM–4 PM. The park is closed on Tues. More information about the park can be found at www.aacounty.org/RecParks/parks/quietwaters.

Kayaks, canoes, stand-up paddleboards, and bicycles can be rented at the park through Paddle or Pedal. They also offer kayak paddling lessons and sunset tours. More information can be found on their Web site at www.paddleorpedal.com, or by calling 410-991-4268.

Length of Paddle: 3–5½ miles; 1½–2½ hours

Route Description

This particular paddle is probably one of the best beginner-intermediate routes in the book. There are about 2 miles of protected waters with interesting cuts to explore, as well as direct access to the wide South River for practicing your stroke in more challenging conditions.

The put-in site is a couple of hundred yards from the closest place to park, down a gently sloping hill, so unless you have a cart to transport your kayak, it is recommended to rent a boat at the boathouse adjacent to the floating-dock launch site.

Once you leave the floating dock, head right, paralleling Quiet Waters Park land. While this side of the waterway is pristine and undeveloped, the far bank is populated with homes and their associated large sail- and motorboats. As you approach the first bend to the right, you will encounter some small square baskets held afloat with PVC tubing and joined together. These are oyster gardens, part of the Chesapeake Bay Foundation's effort to revive the endangered native oyster. For decades, oysters have been the most valuable commodity in the bay; however, today the native oyster population has been estimated at 1 percent of historic levels. Oysters are not only a delectable item in the American diet, they are critical to the health of the bay's fragile ecosystem. They are one of nature's most important purifiers, filtering algae, sand, and pollutants, and their reefs provide a habitat for a wide variety of fish and crabs.

Restoration is critical to help improve the bay's water quality, and the Chesapeake Bay Foundation has several programs for citizens and students to grow oysters along their docks or in protected waters close to shore. The oysters are raised over the course of about one year from juveniles (called spat) to their adult size, usually 1 to 2 inches in length, and then turned back over to the foundation to be transplanted on restored sanctuary reefs.

Continue curving around to the right in a near U turn. Even though, overall, a relatively large number of homes line the waterfront, compared to many of the paddles in this book, there is still a surprising amount and variety of wildlife to observe. We have seen two species

Chesapeake Bay Foundation oyster gardens

of hawks soaring overhead (red-tailed and Cooper's), ospreys, great blue herons, hooded mergansers, mallards, and kingfishers.

Ospreys are one of the most common raptors you will encounter in the area during the spring through fall months; in the winter, most migrate to Florida, the Caribbean, and South America. One of the loudest birds of prey, ospreys will let you know when you get too close, particularly when they are guarding their young. They are true scavengers when they are building their nests, using everything from plastic bags and bottles to fishing line, rope, and other refuse as nesting material, although the majority of the nest is made with sticks and branches. The babies typically fledge about 50 to 60 days after they hatch, and they learn to catch fish in a few weeks, mostly by watching their siblings and parents. The young will normally remain in their nests until September, when they embark on their first migration south.

The waterway here continues to neck down, and you can follow it for about ¾ mile before turning around. Paddling back toward the launch site, one option is to stay to the right side of the waterway where you can see up close all of the large sail- and motorboats and exchange greetings with folks out on their docks.

Just across from the launch site is a piling with an osprey nest on top. Here, you have the choice of staying right and heading out to the open waters of the South River, or cutting back across past the launch site and continuing to explore the protected waters of the park. If you choose the latter, you will find several cuts to paddle in and out of and will see people hiking and walking their dogs on the numerous trails in Quiet Waters Park, as well as additional oyster garden baskets in the water.

If you decide to head out to the South River, you have multiple options for extending your route. The river is about ½ mile wide at this point. Heading left will take you out toward the Chesapeake Bay (3 miles downstream); heading left will take you up the South River with the Solomon Island Road Bridge 2½ miles away. In both directions, there are cuts and inlets to explore, and it is recommended to stay along the riverbanks to avoid the boating traffic in the river.

Ospreys in nest

2.

Clopper Lake, Seneca Creek State Park

Directions: From I-495 (beltway), take I-270 north toward Frederick, Maryland. Take exit 10, MD 117 (Clopper Road). Turn right at the light at the bottom of the ramp. The park is approximately 2 miles on the left. The park entrance fee is $5 per person for noncounty residents.

GPS Coordinates: 39° 08' 37" N; 77° 15' 02" W

Amenities/History: Seneca Creek State Park, covering 6,300 acres along Seneca Creek, has a wide variety of recreational activities including over 16 miles of road/mountain bike and hiking trails, a volleyball court, a Frisbee disc golf course, and a recycled-tire playground. One of these trails, the Greenway Trail, can be followed from the park about 14 miles to Riley's Lock on the C&O Canal. The Maryland State Forest and Park Service and the Friends of Seneca Creek State Park (a volunteer nonprofit organization dedicated to preserving and maintaining the recreational activities of the park), created the trail in 1994, relying completely on volunteer efforts.

The park, which includes forests, fields, streams, and wetlands, is home to a variety of wildlife, including white-tailed deer, fox, wild turkey, and raccoons. In addition, over 200 species of birds have been observed in the park, making it one of the prime birding areas in the National Capital Region.

The boat center on the 90-acre Clopper Lake rents kayaks, canoes, rowboats, and paddleboats in season, May through

September. Kayak lessons are available through Potomac Kayaking, which offers a series of three group courses covering essential paddling skills with an emphasis on safety (www .potomackayaking.com). There is also a restored 19th century cabin and a self-guided path that interprets the history of the area.

The name *Seneca* (Algonkian for "people of the standing rock") comes from the Seneca Indian tribe, the largest of the original five tribes that made up the Iroquois League (along with the Mohawk, the Oneida, the Onondaga, and the Cayuga tribes). In 1722, the Tuscarora joined the league, and it became known as the League of Six Nations. The league still exists, and there are nearly 10,000 Seneca living today in western New York, Kentucky, and Ontario, Canada.

The first European settlers arrived from the mainland in the late 1600s and found an abundance of natural resources, including fertile soil rich in nutrients to farm, mature forests for building materials, and a huge variety of fish and game to provide sustenance. The many streams in the region also provided power for two of the main historic remnants still standing today, the Black Rock and Clopper Mills gristmills. Outdoor exhibits describe the operation of the Black Rock gristmill on Great Seneca Creek.

Length of Paddle: 3 miles (to circumnavigate the lake, including exploring the coves); 1½ hours

Route Description

The car-top-only boat ramp adjacent to the boathouse consists of a sloped section of small concrete blocks and a shallow, muddy section on either side for launching your kayak. There is ample parking, no launch fee, and restrooms and vending machines in the boat center.

This site is ideal for both the beginner kayaker and for paddling with children because of the very clear water along the shoreline, where they can easily spot turtles and fish underwater. Children can paddle a good portion of the lake without too much effort. The wildlife you can expect to encounter includes American kestrels, spotted sandpipers,

Clopper Lake launch site

herons, cormorants, barn swallows, and a variety of ducks. You will also hear bullfrogs and the unique rolling, trilling call of the many red-bellied woodpeckers that inhabit the park. These medium-sized birds are very noticeable because of their striking barred black-and-white backs as well as their red crests. Their name is a slight misnomer, however, as their crests are redder than their bellies, and they are often confused with the rarer red-headed woodpecker, a close relative whose entire head is, indeed, a bright red.

Depending on the time of year, you will also be treated to some beautiful vegetation along the banks, including blackberry bushes, swamp lilies, mountain laurel, foxglove, and dogwood and swamp maple trees.

The lake has a few coves to explore, and as you approach the ends

Red-bellied woodpecker

of these coves and the area where Seneca Creek flows into the lake (to the left of the launch point, there is a DO NOT ENTER sign over the sluice gate that marks the entrance to the creek), be aware of multiple submerged and exposed logs. In the spring through summer months, all sizes of turtles come out to sun themselves on the logs, ranging in size from 2 inches to just over 1 foot. This paddle contains by far the most turtles we have seen on any of the routes in this book. It is also one of the more popular fishing spots in Montgomery County, where anglers can expect to find largemouth bass, bluegill, catfish, and tiger muskie accessible either from the path that encircles the lake or from inexpensive rowboats for rent.

Blackberry flower

The other feature of the lake, at the far end from Seneca Creek, is an earthen dam on the Long Draught Branch River. The dam was built in 1975 for recreation and flood control and is topped by Seneca Creek Road. Just to the right and before you reach the open field/picnic area near the launch site is evidence of a beaver lodge.

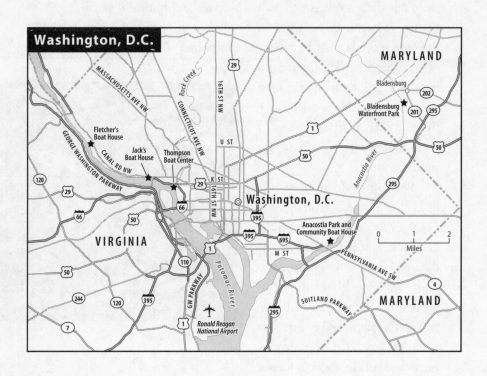

Washington, D.C.

MARYLAND

Bladensburg

Bladensburg
Waterfront Park

Fletcher's
Boat House

Jack's
Boat House

Thompson
Boat Center

Washington, D.C.

Anacostia Park and
Community Boat House

VIRGINIA

Ronald Reagan
National Airport

MARYLAND

MASSACHUSETTS AVE NW

Rock Creek

16TH ST NW

CONNECTICUT AVE NW

GEORGE WASHINGTON PARKWAY

CANAL RD NW

U ST

K ST

16TH ST NW

M ST

GW PARKWAY

Potomac River

PENNSYLVANIA AVE SW

SUITLAND PARKWAY

Anacostia River

Miles

0   1   2

Washington, D.C.

3.

Potomac River: Thompson Boat Center

Directions: From I-66 in Virginia, cross Roosevelt Bridge and get into the left-most lane. Follow the signs toward Whitehurst Freeway and Rock Creek Parkway. After ¼ mile, the road splits into two left and two right lanes; stay in the left lanes. Turn left at the intersection heading toward the Watergate Complex, then turn right onto Virginia Avenue. Get in the left lane and cross over Rock Creek Parkway at the green light and turn into the parking lot on the right. Thompson Boat Center is across a small walking bridge and to the left.

An alternative launch site is Jack's Boat House. From Virginia, cross over the Rosslyn-Key Bridge into Georgetown and turn right on M Street. Continue to Wisconsin Avenue, and turn right. Follow Wisconsin Avenue to the T intersection at the Georgetown Waterfront Park (the largest public park constructed in Washington, D.C.). Turn right on Water Street (you will be driving under the Whitehurst Freeway), and Jack's Boathouse is about 100 yards up on the left, just past the Key Bridge overpass.

GPS Coordinates: Thompson Boat Center—38° 54' 00"; 77° 03' 30" W; Jack's Boathouse—38° 54' 14" N; 77° 04' 12" W

Amenities: Thompson Boat Center is one of the best launching spots along the Potomac River in downtown Washington in terms of variety of scenery and flexibility. The center rents canoes and kayaks from mid-March through the end of October (but you can launch your own kayaks there year-round), so it's ideal for an outing with friends or visitors that don't have touring kayaks. Adjacent to both the Kennedy Center and Georgetown, it is ideally situated for short to longer-range paddles of both pristine shoreline upriver and cityscape-monument views downriver. The boat center also rents bicycles in season. At Jack's Boat House, there are no restrooms, and he charges $10 per kayak to launch from his floating docks.

Length of Paddle: 4½–6½ miles; 2–3 hours

Route Description

Depending on the time of day and time of year, you will invariably see sprint canoeists and rowers in sculls from singles all the way to eight-person teams with coxswains. This particular stretch of the Potomac, from about 3,000 yards upriver of the boat center to 2,500 yards downriver, brackets the stretch of river that is the training and competition course for multiple college and high school crew teams. Also, in May of each year, the Washington, D.C., Dragon Boat festival is held along this stretch (see sidebar, page 30).

Thompson Boat Center with Kennedy Center in the background

Paddling upriver from the boathouse, you will pass several of the tonier waterfront restaurants and shops that make up the Georgetown Waterfront Harbor complex along the right bank. There are several places to tie up your kayak and stop in for a lunch or beverage, either heading upriver or on the return trip. Just past the harbor is the newly renovated Georgetown Waterfront Park, opened in 2010 and managed by the National Park Service. You will then paddle under the Key Bridge, and Jack's Boathouse is just beyond the bridge on the right bank.

Next up is the Washington Canoe Club (www.washingtoncanoe club.org) on the right, where canoeists have been paddling since 1904. The club has placed athletes on almost every Canoe/Kayak Olympic Team since 1924, when Flatwater Sprint Canoeing was introduced as a demonstration sport. While there is normally a 1- to 3–knot, downriver current in this stretch of the river, even the most novice of kayakers will be able to paddle against it without too much additional effort.

Along the left bank of the river, the George Washington Memorial Parkway parallels the river, but the mostly kudzu vegetation along the banks masks the majority of both the traffic and the road noise. As you continue upriver, with the Capital Crescent Trail and C&O Canal Tow-path along the right bank, you will leave the hustle and bustle of the city behind and paddle along a stretch of the river that is surprisingly devoid of human habitation, with the exception of bicyclers and joggers on the bike trails.

We have seen a family of deer in February, along with great blue herons, eagles, ospreys, red-tailed hawks, various species of ducks, and the gregarious cedar waxwings throughout the year.

Cedar waxwings, which get their name from their fondness for the small cones of the eastern red cedar tree, are very social creatures, often fly-

Cedar waxwing
IMAGE COURTESY OF GUS RAY

The Three Sisters formation in the Potomac River

ing in flocks of more than 50 birds. They are distinguished by their high, thin whistles and are often seen flying over the water in search of insects. While they look similar to female cardinals, their bodies are stockier. The adults have masked beaks, pale, yellow bellies, and red, waxlike spots on the wings.

As you continue upriver, you will come to a series of rock formations in the middle of the river. These are known as the Three Sisters (or the Three Sisters Island), and they represent the farthest point navigable by most larger boats. In the warmer months, you will likely see multiple pleasure boats moored together and anchored just downriver from the formation.

There are several legends about the Three Sisters, but one of the best tells of three Native American women who tried to escape a chieftain pursuing them by swimming across the river. They drowned and were turned into the three island rocks by the Great Spirit. It is said that Native Americans crafted the legend to warn their children of the danger in even the calm Potomac River currents in this stretch.

Along with a surprisingly diverse amount of flora and wildlife here, boulders and rocks populate the riverbed here, just below the surface.

Along either shoreline, depending on the water conditions and sunlight, you can see several feet below the surface and spot not only the boulders transported downriver over the millennium but medium to large smallmouth bass and other game fish as well.

Washington, D.C., Dragon Boat Festival

Dragon boat races trace their heritage to ancient China, 2,500 years ago, when the first races were held on the Yangtze River. The sport did not expand beyond China's borders, however, until 1970, when Hong Kong staged the first International Dragon Boat Race to promote its culture.

Now, more than 50 million people compete in races around the world, and it is one of the fastest growing water sports in the country. Each crew consists of 20 paddlers, 1 drummer, and 1 steersperson, and the boats are painted bright colors to resemble dragon scales with equally colorful dragon heads on the bows and tails on the sterns of the boats. Typically, races are held over distances of between 200 and 2,000 meters, with the racing divided between festival (fun) and premier (competitive) categories. The Washington, D.C., festival usually draws about 60 teams each year. More information can be found at www.dragonboatdc.com.

Dragon Boat races

Rosslyn Key Bridge and the Washington Monument

Farther upriver, on the left bank, are two waterfalls that cascade down from incoming tributaries below the George Washington Memorial Parkway. Like most river paddles, we recommend paddling alongside both banks throughout the length of the traverse to take advantage of the variety in scenery. Turning around at this point and returning to the boat center is about a 4½-mile paddle.

For a longer paddle, you can stay along the right bank, as you pass back under Key Bridge and circumnavigate Theodore Roosevelt Island to the right (described in chapter 7), passing under the pedestrian bridge and then the I-66 bridge (twice, on either side of the island), before returning to the launch point, which makes for about a 6½-mile journey.

4.

Potomac River: Fletcher's Boat House

Directions: Fletcher's Boat House is located 2 miles north of Key Bridge and 1 mile south of Chain Bridge (on the Washington, D.C., side), at the intersection of Reservoir and Canal Roads. You will know you have reached the entrance to Fletcher's when you see the Abner Cloud House, an old stone building adjacent to the canal. From I-495 (beltway), take exit 41, Glen Echo. You will be on the Clara Barton Parkway. Follow the parkway until it becomes Canal Road at Chain Bridge. Continue on Canal Road until the entrance of Fletcher's Boat House at Canal and Reservoir Roads is on the right. From I-66 east, take exit 73, Rosslyn, to Key Bridge. After crossing over Key Bridge, take a left onto Canal Road. Bear left at Foxhall Road to stay on Canal Road, and continue to the entrance of Fletcher's Cove at Canal and Reservoir on the left.

GPS Coordinates: 38° 55' 02" N; 77° 06' 08"

Amenities: Fletcher's Boat House has provided kayak, canoe, and boat rentals for decades and has been one of the premier recreational and fishing spots in Washington, D.C., for over a century. Situated along the C&O Canal and the Capital Crescent Trail, it is also a perfect spot for biking, walking, and running. Information on recreation activities and rentals can be found at www.fletchersboathouse.com.

Although the boathouse has several floating docks for launching their rental boats, they don't allow private craft to launch from these docks. Drive down to the end of the long dirt parking lot and launch along the small rock and gravel shoreline to the right. There is no launch fee, and there are restroom facilities at the boathouse.

Length of Paddle: $2\frac{3}{4}$–$4\frac{1}{2}$ miles; $1\frac{1}{4}$–$2\frac{1}{4}$ hours

Route Description

You will have to carry your kayak about 40 yards from the parking lot to the launch site. Since this paddle is just downstream of Great and Little Falls, there is a relatively strong current, and it's recommended to go upriver first to make sure you have enough endurance to make the return trip. Heading upriver toward Chain Bridge, you will begin to encounter submerged and partially exposed boulders, which have been deposited over centuries of Potomac River floods. The water is crystal clear here, and you can see several feet to the river's bottom. The forested area along the towpath to the right is home to many families of deer and fox, and you can often see these animals foraging along the shoreline.

Fletcher's Boat House launch site

Canal History

Fletcher's Boat House has been in existence since the 1850s, but the canal traces its history back to 1785, when George Washington was appointed president of the Potomack Company in charge of canal construction. The canal was to make the Potomac River navigable from Cumberland, Maryland, 184 miles to the northwest, to Georgetown, and the major engineering challenge was traversing the treacherous Great Falls section just upriver from the location of the boathouse. It is said Washington had two obsessions, continually improving his family's Mount Vernon home (described in the section on Little Hunting Creek) and making the Potomac River navigable around Great Falls. Even after he was elected our first president, he was still involved with the project to the point that he loaned the company money in 1798 to complete the Great Falls Locks. Washington passed away, however, in 1799, three years before the canal's completion in 1802.

Also located here is the historic Abner Cloud House, the oldest house on the canal. Abner Cloud was a miller who built the house and mill in 1801 to take advantage of the transport access the canal provided for his flour downstream to the Georgetown markets.

Abner Cloud historic house

As you approach Chain Bridge, approximately 1 mile from the launch point, you will encounter a stronger current, the result of the first set of rapids that make up the Little Falls section of the Potomac. Paddling under the bridge, you will see steep cliffs along the left bank with some of the most beautiful and expensive domains of the Washington elite perched above.

This first set of rapids, about ½ mile from Chain Bridge, is the farthest upriver touring kayaks can be paddled, and you will frequently encounter whitewater paddlers practicing their skills or returning to Fletcher's after traversing the upriver falls. This section of the Potomac River, encompassing both Little Falls and Great Falls, is one of the premier whitewater kayaking spots in the world with multiple class 5-plus drops. Paddlers training for both the Olympics and other world and national competitions often hone their skills on these stretches, with names like Rocky Island Rapids, Wet Bottom Chute, and Difficult Run Rapids.

Heading back downriver, the opposite bank (on the other side from Fletcher's Boat House) contains popular picnic areas and hiking paths accessible from both a parking lot near Chain Bridge as well as several pull-offs along the George Washington Memorial Parkway, which at this point rises about 200 feet above the river. Eagles and ospreys can often be sited soaring above the river here and alighting in the tallest of the trees along the parkway. There are a couple of small but pretty waterfalls nestled in among the trees and kudzu, and kingfishers are prevalent, skittering up and down among the trees along the shoreline.

Osprey

One of the best-kept secrets for enjoying the outdoors in our nation's capital are the two parks along George Washington Memorial Parkway: Fort Marcy and Turkey Run. The combination of Civil War–era artifacts and earthworks, extensive network of hiking and running trails, and picnicking areas is nearly unmatched anywhere in the area.

Each park has a ¼-mile trail that connects to the Potomac Heritage Trail along the river. This trail is a portion of the 830-mile network of locally managed trails that extend from the mouth of the Chesapeake Bay up to the Allegheny highlands in the Ohio River basin. The 8½-mile section of the trail here is a wonderful, easy-to-moderate hike from Roosevelt Island across from Georgetown upriver to the American Legion Bridge (part of the I-495 beltway). There is ample parking adjacent to the Roosevelt Island walking bridge.

Turkey Run Park is also near both the George Washington Parkway Headquarters and the Claude Moore Colonial Farm, a working re-creation of a small 1700s tobacco farm. The farm is open April through mid-December.

For a shorter paddle (about 2¾ miles), return to the launch point. To extend this route, continue downriver past Fletcher's Boat House on the left. Depending on the time of year, you will most likely encounter both boaters fishing for the abundant largemouth and striped bass and catfish in the river, as well as intrepid single scullers (rowers in racing shells) and racing canoeists up from one of the many boathouses in Georgetown. Also along the left shore, high above the river and the corresponding Capital Crescent Trail is the 50-acre Dalecarlia Reservoir, the primary storage reservoir for drinking water in Washington, D.C. Depending on your time available and stamina, you can turn around at this point or extend the paddle farther downriver before returning to the launch site.

5.

Anacostia River: Anacostia Park and Community Boat House

Directions: To get to the Anacostia Community Boat House from points south (Virginia), take I-395 north to the Sixth Street exit. Continue straight on Virginia Avenue; turn right on Eighth Street, left on M Street, and continue under the Pennsylvania Avenue Bridge (formally the John Philip Sousa Bridge) to 1000 M Street.

An alternate launch site is Anacostia Park Boat Ramp, on the far side of the Anacostia River, which can be used when you can't launch from the boathouse (regattas, closed events). To get to the boat ramp, follow I-395 north into Washington, D.C., toward the Southeast–Southwest Freeway. Stay left, and follow the signs for I-295 south (Anacostia Freeway) and Pennsylvania Avenue. Exit onto Pennsylvania Avenue and cross the bridge, taking the first right onto Fairlawn Avenue. Go to the stop sign, and turn right again on Nicholson Street to enter the park. Turn right and continue past the skating pavilion and tennis court area to the boat ramp on the left. There are restroom facilities near the skating pavilion.

GPS Coordinates: Anacostia Community Boat House—38° 52' 42.5" N; 76° 58' 31.0"

Amenities: At the Community Boat House, there are wide aluminum boat ramps (you can carry two kayaks abreast) that lead to several floating docks, primarily used by rowing and canoe racing clubs. There is no launch fee, and there are restroom facilities in the boathouse.

Length of Paddle: 4¼–8 miles; 2–3½ hours

Route Description

This is one of the more surprising paddles in the book; it's hard to imagine there is this much tranquility and beauty nestled in the middle of northeast Washington, D.C.

The lower portion of the Anacostia River is also part of the Captain John Smith Chesapeake National Historic Trail. Between 1607 and 1609, Captain John Smith explored and mapped nearly 3,000 miles of the Chesapeake Bay and many of its major tributaries. In 2007, to commemorate this amazing feat and as part of the 400th anniversary of the founding of Jamestown, Congress established America's first national water trail.

Once a tributary is designated as a water trail component, the National Park Service then works closely with state and local agencies and other conservation and tribal organizations to provide financial assistance in support of conservation efforts, resource management, and facility maintenance along these waterways. Other waterways that compose this trail, included in this book, are the Potomac, Patuxent, Occoquan, and Mattaponi Rivers.

Tributaries are added to the water trail based on an evaluation and research conducted by the Chesapeake Conservancy. In May 2012, the National Park Service added four new components: the Susquehanna, Chester, the Upper Nanticoke, and the Upper James Rivers, bringing the total length of trails to over 3,000 miles. More information about the trail can be found at www.nps.gov/cajo/index.htm.

While the Anacostia River played a major role in the founding of our nation's capital and in the War of 1812, perhaps it is most well known for its unfortunate status as one of the nation's most neglected and abused urban waterways, after centuries of pollution by-products found their way into the river from industrial, residential, and agricultural sources. However, the Anacostia is slowly rebounding. Antiquated sewage systems are being eliminated, and the federal government is implementing a storm-water management program, aimed at improving the quality of the water in the river. Hundreds of acres of wetlands are being restored, and miles of trees and other vegetation now line the

Anacostia Boat House launch site

river as buffers. Significant numbers of aquatic grasses, clams, and mussels, which are some of nature's most efficient water filterers, are emerging as well.

Whether departing from the boathouse or Anacostia Park, head upriver under the railroad bridge access (low clearance) toward RFK stadium in the distance, on the left bank. In about ½ mile, you will notice a narrow entrance on the left side of the river flanked by two large cement structures on the left bank. This marks the southern extent of Lake Kingman. Paddling through this entrance (or, you can paddle to the right of the entrance as well) puts you on the left side of Kingman Island, the first of two islands you will encounter on this route.

The U.S. Army Corps of Engineers created these two islands, as well as Lake Kingman, at the turn of the 20th century, and the 45-acre restoration project is now an excellent habitat for numerous bird and fish species, as well as reptiles and mammals.

Just inside the entrance, you will begin to notice the first of many of the wetlands in the river park in the waters adjacent to both banks. These can be identified by both the large stands of cattails and other

Entrance to Kingman Lake

marsh grasses and also 3- to 4-foot-high fenced-in areas. The fenced-in areas are part of the Anacostia Watershed Society's Rice Rangers Program, where students grow plants in the classroom and then transplant them into the tidal marshes. Nearly all the Anacostia wetlands have been destroyed over the past several decades, and this is one of several efforts the society has made to restore and clean up the river.

After passing under the Whitney Young Memorial (vehicle) Bridge (adjacent to RFK Stadium), stay left, paddling to the left of Heritage Island. You will then come upon a low-clearance boardwalk across the lake, which provides foot access to both Kingman and Heritage islands. Each has a walking/cycling trail and outdoor classroom areas. Additional information about this beautiful recreational area can be found at www.kingmanisland.org.

Farther along, after passing under the footbridge to Heritage Island, you will pass under the Ethel Kennedy Bridge and the more elevated Metro (subway) bridge for the Orange line. On either side of the waterway here is the Langston Golf Course; golfing is another recreational activity available as part of Anacostia Park. There will be multiple, tidal-marsh, fenced areas to navigate through, and unfortunately, many of the enclosures appear to be collection areas for discarded bottles and other debris. We have flushed several wood ducks here and have observed ospreys and great blue herons fishing in this area as well. About ¾ mile past the two bridges, you will paddle under a golf cart bridge, which marks the northern extend of Kingman Island. Turn to the right and head back downriver toward the launch point.

Along the left bank, you will notice the five tall stacks and multiple smaller cooling towers of the Potomac Electric Power Plant on the left bank. Shortly past the power plant, we once noticed four deer swimming across the river from Kingman Island to the mainland. They had to jump over one of the tidal marsh restoration fences before reaching land, and then they bounded along the shoreline in front of the power plant. Just past this point is an exposed boulder near the left bank, which makes a perfect location for cormorants to sun themselves and dry their wings. After a slight bend to the right, you will see the railroad bridge where the paddle began.

Resting cormorants

Washington Navy Yard and USS *Barry*

The Washington Navy Yard has long served as one of the ceremonial gateways to the nation's capital, hosting diplomatic missions as far back as a Japanese delegation in 1860. It was also the site where the body of the Unknown Soldier from World War I was received and where Charles Lindbergh returned after his transatlantic flight. Today, the navy yard serves as headquarters for the Naval District Washington and contains the Naval Sea Systems Command, as well as numerous support activities. The yard is also home to an impressive Navy Museum, housing artifacts from the Revolutionary War through to the present day. Around the grounds of the yard are 26 bronze guns and cannons made by the United States, Spain, France, and Italy and used in various conflicts in the 17th through 19th centuries, dating back to a 1686 Spanish 6-pounder.

The USS *Barry* (DD 933) is a Forrest Sherman–class destroyer, commissioned in September 1956 and named after the Revolutionary War hero, Commodore John Barry. She saw service in Vietnam, earning two battle stars, and was also part of the task force that blockaded Cuba when the United States found evidence that the Soviet Union had installed missiles on the island. She was decommissioned in 1982, and in 1984, the ship was permanently anchored at the Washington Navy Yard. Today, the USS *Barry* is used in naval ceremonies and also serves as a platform for training and shipboard familiarization.

USS Barry

To extend your paddle, continue south past the boathouse. In about 300 yards, you will pass under the John Philip Sousa Bridge, and in another 300 yards will be the first of three private yacht clubs along the right shore. Just past the next two bridges (11th Street and Officer Kevin Welsh Memorial), the river bends to the right, and you will come upon the seawall that delineates the historic Washington Navy Yard, the U.S. Navy's longest continuously operated federal facility.

Turning around at this point would constitute a 7-mile paddle. However, by continuing another ½ mile, you will come to the Washington Nationals baseball stadium and the adjoining and newly developed Yards Park, which includes open grassy areas, a waterfall and fountain area with a wading pool, a terraced lawn performance venue, recreational trails, and riverside gardens with restaurants and shops.

6.

Anacostia River: Bladensburg Waterfront Park

Directions: From Washington, D.C., take New York Avenue east. Turn north on Bladensburg Road and pass Peace Cross on the left. You are now on MD 450. Take the first right into Bladensburg Waterfront Park. There is a sign at the entrance.

From Maryland, take I-495 (beltway), exit 23 to MD 201 south (Kenilworth Avenue) toward Bladensburg. Go 5 miles, and after the traffic light for Upshur Street intersection, go right on the exit ramp to MD 450 (Annapolis Road). Turn left at the end of the exit ramp onto MD 450 west, and the park entrance is two blocks on the left.

From Virginia, take MD 201 north (Kenilworth Avenue), also I-295 north. Take the exit ramp on the right to MD 450 west. Turn left at the stoplight onto MD 450 west. The park entrance is two blocks on the left.

GPS Coordinates: 38° 56' 00" N; 76° 56' 19" W

Amenities: This is a terrific launch site with several floating docks, restroom facilities, vending machines, plenty of parking, and signage interpreting the rich history of the area. There is no launch fee, and you can rent kayaks and canoes for $8 per hour or $20 per day (nonresident), from late May to early October. The site provides kayak-paddling lessons during boathouse open hours (10 AM–6 PM), and it also serves as the launch site for the University of Maryland and Catholic University rowing clubs.

The Bladensburg Waterfront Park and the Kenilworth Aquatic Gardens, the destination for this paddle, are part of the Anacostia River Water Trail, which highlights several historical and recreational sites along the river, from Magruder Park in the north to the river's confluence with the Potomac River in the south. For more information about the water trail, go to www.anacostiaws.org/images/maps/AnacostiaRiverWater TrailGuide.pdf.

Length of Paddle: 5–7½ miles; 2¼–3½ hours

Route Description

The Anacostia River, about 9 miles long, has a long and varied history. It is believed that Native Americans lived on the river for 10,000 years. The Nacotchtank Indians called it Anaquash, which means "village trading center." In the late 18th century, the water depth was between 25 and 30 feet, and the river was an important commercial trade route, particularly for farm crops such as tobacco, corn, and cotton. By the late 1800s, however, the depth decreased to between 10 and 15 feet, mainly due to increased silting from runoff and sewage discharge into the river.

Bladensburg Waterfront Park launch site

Today, the average depth of the river is about 6 feet at Bladensburg and 20 feet at the confluence with the Potomac River. The river along this stretch has a 3-foot tidal difference, one of the largest tidal differences in the Chesapeake Bay watershed, and it's best to paddle at or near high tide to maximize your accessibility to the shallow waters of the adjoining Kenilworth Aquatic Gardens.

Departing from the boat dock, head left downriver on this long, relatively straight stretch that is about 80 to 90 yards across. Along the left bank is the Anacostia Riverwalk Trail, a 16-mile multiuse trail connecting the National Mall at the Tidal Basin to the Bladensburg Waterfront Park. Beyond the trail along this bank and farther up on the right bank are stands of restored wetlands and cattails that are critical to the river's ecosystem and its survival. While there is a narrow tributary along the right bank about ¾ mile from the launch point that can be accessed at high tide, it's best to save this for the return trip to ensure you have the endurance to extend your route.

This is a very peaceful stretch of the river with dense forests on both banks, the tranquility broken only by the vehicles crossing over the New York Avenue Bridge and nearby railroad bridge, about another ¼ mile past the tributary. Besides the numerous swallows that make their homes under the railroad bridge, ospreys, herons, woodpeckers, geese, turtles, and the occasional river otter can also be observed here.

Just past the bridges on the left bank is the start of a low, block seawall that continues for another ½ mile up to a gap in the bank that marks the entrance to the Kenilworth Aquatic Gardens. This is the only national park in the country devoted to cultivating water-loving plants, and while it can be enjoyed on foot along the many walking trails, seeing it up close by boat is a special experience.

Tree swallow in birdhouse

History of Kenilworth Aquatic Gardens

Shortly after the end of the Civil war, Walter Shaw, a retired war veteran, purchased 37 acres of marshland along the Anacostia River to pursue his hobby and passion, the growing of water lilies. He continued to dig additional ponds and experimented with crossing a variety of lilies to create new strains, and along with his daughter, Helen Shaw Fowler, created a very successful business shipping thousands of over 60 varieties of lilies daily to some of the nation's major cities.

In the 1930s, the lower Anacostia River was so filled with silt, the U.S. Army Corps of Engineers had to dredge this part of the river, and Helen Shaw was forced to fight to keep the Shaw Gardens from being filled in by the dredged material. In 1938, Congress passed legislation to protect eight acres of gardens, which then came under the national park system as a component of Anacostia Park. The gardens have essentially remained unchanged since then, and today thousands of visitors and professional and amateur photographers flock here annually to enjoy a true national treasure.

After entering the narrow opening to the gardens, you can choose to paddle either direction around the first of numerous small islands, this one with a swallow birdhouse on it. While there are 75 types of swallows worldwide, only 8 live in the United States and Canada.

The gardens are an impressive paddling destination year-round, but late May through August is when the water lilies and lotus flowers the park is famous for are in bloom. Also, it's best to plan for an early morning

Water lilies, Kenilworth Aquatic Gardens

*Lotus flower, Kenilworth
Aquatic Gardens*

paddle before the flowers close up for the day in response to the heat. While many people consider water lilies and lotus flowers to be one and the same, there are two easy ways to distinguish between the two. Water lilies sit on the water and have multiple filaments in the center of their flower, and lotus flowers have a single barrel shaped carpel (female part) in their center and rise above the water. To find out what is in bloom at any particular time of year, you can contact an aquatic gardens park ranger at 202-426-6905. The 14-acre site contains numerous connected and isolated ponds, and it's about 1¼-mile paddle to explore all of the navigable water.

To extend your route, after exiting the gardens, turn left, downriver, and paddle about ¾ mile to the northern tip of Kingman Island (and the northern extent of the Anacostia Park route in this book), distinguishable by the golf cart bridge to the right for the Langston Golf Course, before turning around.

A second alternative is to head back to the launch site and continue upriver, passing under the iron walking/cycling bridge and the Bladensburg Road Bridge, until you come to a fork; stay to the right (the river narrows to about 20 to 30 yards across here), and paddle under the Baltimore Avenue Bridge for another ½ mile until you come to a railroad bridge and the turnaround point. The hustle and bustle of northeast Washington, D.C., in this stretch is in stark contrast to the previous portion of the route.

Virginia

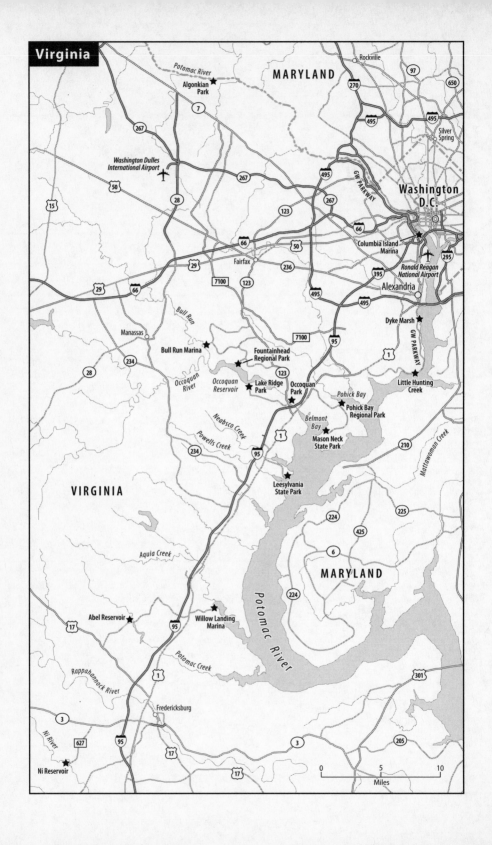

Virginia

MARYLAND

Rockville

97

650

270

495

495

Silver Spring

Potomac River

Algonkian Park

7

267

Washington Dulles International Airport

50

15

28

267

123

495

GW PARKWAY

Washington D.C.

267

66

Columbia Island Marina

Ronald Reagan National Airport

295

50

236

395

29

Fairfax

7100

123

Alexandria

29

66

495

495

Bull Run

7100

95

Dyke Marsh

GW PARKWAY

Manassas

1

234

Bull Run Marina

Fountainhead Regional Park

Little Hunting Creek

28

Occoquan River

Occoquan Reservoir

123

Lake Ridge Park

Occoquan Park

Pohick Bay

Pohick Bay Regional Park

Neabsco Creek

Belmont Bay

Mason Neck State Park

210

Mattawoman Creek

Powells Creek

234

1

95

Leesylvania State Park

225

VIRGINIA

224

425

Aquia Creek

6

MARYLAND

224

Potomac River

Abel Reservoir

Willow Landing Marina

95

17

95

Potomac Creek

301

Rappahannock River

1

3

Fredericksburg

205

Ni River

627

95

3

17

Ni Reservoir

17

0   5   10

Miles

7.

Potomac River: Columbia Island Marina

Directions: The put-in site is at the Columbia Island Marina, just north of Ronald Reagan National Airport along the George Washington Memorial Parkway, located near Lady Bird Johnson Park and LBJ Memorial Grove. If coming from the north along the parkway, turn right into Columbia Island Marina. If coming from the south, you must take the Arlington Cemetery exit off the parkway and make a U turn at the traffic circle in order to be in the southbound lane and make the right turn into the marina.

GPS Coordinates: 38° 52' 30" N; 77° 02' 59" W

Amenities: You can launch kayaks at the boat ramp for free, but during peak boating season in the summer, there can sometimes be short delays due to the many boats and recreational vehicles that are launched and recovered there. The marina has restroom facilities and a small snack bar adjacent to the boat ramp.

Length of Paddle: 1½–2¾ hours; 3½–6½ miles

Route Description

While this particular route (mostly along the Potomac River) bisects the National Mall in Washington, D.C., to the north and Arlington, Virginia, to the south, and the put-in site is less than 200 yards from the Pentagon, it has become our favorite paddle for a few reasons. It includes paddling in very narrow passages as well as open waters; we have never failed to see a variety of interesting wildlife and vegetation; you have multiple options to extend your route to up to an entire day paddle; and at particular times of the year, you can paddle near multiple high school and college rowing crews practicing their skills and observe up close dragon boat races (described below).

This is one of the few paddles where you have to take the tides into account to maximize your experience. To make it through the cut without portaging your kayak, you should plan to launch two hours either side of high tide. After you launch and clear the boat docks, depending on the wind direction, head either right up the cut or left past the Pentagon and exit out to the Potomac River to the left and under Humpback Bridge (George Washington Memorial Parkway). Along the cut, you will encounter a variety of wildlife, including many shorebirds (ducks, terns, and herons—night, green, and great blue), birds of prey (ospreys and eagles), turtles, and the occasional muskrat or beaver.

Even though the cut and Columbia Island are in between two major highways, US 27 and the George Washington Memorial Parkway, we have seen both deer and a family of foxes on the shoreline! We have

Columbia Island Marina boat ramp

Turtles sunning in the cut

paddled out of Columbia Island Marina probably over 50 times and have never failed to encounter interesting wildlife. You will paddle under four bridges along the cut: one walking bridge from the Virginia mainland to Columbia Island and Lady Bird Johnson Park, two "bison" bridges, two steel and concrete road bridges (VA 27 and the parkway), and the northern extent of the Mount Vernon bike trail paralleling the parkway. The bison bridges are distinguished by their 6-foot-tall bison keystones sculpted by Alexander Phimister Proctor in the 1920s, under the direction of the congressionally authorized Arlington Memorial Bridge Commission.

Once you exit the cut into the Potomac River, depending on how long you want to paddle, you can turn left and circumvent Theodore Roosevelt Island or turn right and head up the Potomac toward Memorial Bridge. Theodore Roosevelt Island, a 90-acre memorial park, is part of the George Washington Memorial Parkway managed by the National Park Service. The Roosevelt Memorial, consisting of a 17-foot-high bronze statue surrounded by large granite tablets with quotes from his writings, was built on the island in the 1960s and dedicated in 1967. The memorial highlights Roosevelt's life and accomplishments as a

Paddling under one of the "bison" bridges

conservationist, naturalist, and outdoorsman. The island park contains 2½ miles of walking trails, and access to it is via a pedestrian footbridge connecting the island with a parking lot along the George Washington Memorial Parkway. The park is open daily, 6 AM–10 PM.

There are several places along the banks of Theodore Roosevelt Island to beach your kayak and take advantage of a wonderfully secluded and pristine park in the middle of one of the world's great cities. A walk around the island, taking in the tributes to Theodore Roosevelt and enjoying the wildlife, can be accomplished in around an hour, or alternatively, there are several beautiful sites for an afternoon picnic.

While the Potomac is fairly wide at this point (about ⅓ mile across from either end of the island), transiting across to the Washington, D.C., side is straightforward and provides a close-up view of the Lincoln Memorial, the Kennedy Center, and the waterfront restaurants of Georgetown (if you choose to paddle past Roosevelt Island). Early spring is a particularly good time of year for this paddle, as the cherry blossoms encircling the tidal basin and many other trees and flowers along the Potomac are in bloom. May is also the month for the annual Dragon Boat Festival, described in detail in chapter 3.

From either side of the Potomac, as you head downriver, you will paddle under Memorial Bridge, one of the most beautiful and historic bridges on the Eastern Seaboard.

Arlington Memorial Bridge, completed in 1932, connects the Lincoln Memorial with Arlington House. The former home of the Confederate General Robert E. Lee, it still stands today on top of the highest point in Arlington Cemetery (and is now a National Park Service memorial site). It is said that the bridge symbolically linked the North and South after the Civil War.

After passing under Memorial Bridge, you can choose to extend the length of this particular trip by paddling on the north side of the river (closer to the D.C. side), passing the entrance to the Tidal Basin and Thomas Jefferson Memorial and along Haines Point, before crossing the Potomac and returning to the marina. For a shorter paddle, remain on the south side of the river until you encounter Humpback Bridge

Potomac River near Roosevelt Island

(about 1 mile past Memorial Bridge) on your right, which marks the entrance back into the Columbia Island basin and the end of this beautiful and historic-themed journey. As you make your way along the basin, you may often encounter one of the DC Ducks, World War II amphibious vehicles that have been restored and converted to sightseeing craft. The company that operates them (www.DCDucks.com) provides a unique 90-minute tour of Washington, D.C., which combines traveling along the main thoroughfares of the city with a river cruise along the Potomac.

8.

Dyke Marsh:
Belle Haven Marina

Directions: From Old Town Alexandria, take Washington Street
south toward Mount Vernon. Washington Street becomes the
George Washington Memorial Parkway. One mile south of Old
Town, look for signs for Dyke Marsh and the Belle Haven Picnic
Area and Marina. Turn left into the park and follow the drive to
the water and the marina office on the right.

From I-495 (beltway), take US 1 south to exit 177A, staying
in the right lane. From the right lane, follow the sign for the left
turn onto Fort Hunt Road. From Fort Hunt Road, turn left on
Belle Haven Road, and follow it until it ends at the George
Washington Memorial Parkway. Turn right, take the first left into
the park, and follow the drive to the water and the marina
office on the right.

GPS Coordinates: 38° 46' 35" N; 77° 02' 55" W

Amenities: The launch area for kayaks is at the end of the drive,
about 40 yards past the marina office. There is a small boat
ramp adjacent to the marina office, but the preferred kayak
launch is at the end of the drive, where you will find a very
shallow, AstroTurf-covered launch ramp. Launch fees are $3 per
kayak, payable at the marina office, and if you keep your
receipts, the fifth launch is free. Kayaks ($25 for two hours)
and canoes can also be rented here, and the marina offers sailing lessons on several varieties of sailboats. There are
restrooms and parking at Belle Haven Park, and restrooms

across the drive from the marina office. The park is also a terrific place to begin a bicycle tour along the George Washington Memorial Parkway bike path to Mount Vernon (a distance of about 11 miles), home of our first president, George Washington.

Length of Paddle: 4–7¾ miles; 1¾–3½ hours

Route Description

This was one of the first paddles we discovered when we took up kayak paddling almost 12 years ago. Its proximity to downtown Washington, D.C., and the diversity of wildlife and fauna make it one of our favorite return spots. While you can make this paddle at any tide, there are spots toward the farthest reaches of the marsh where more water at or near high tide allows you to extend your route.

Leaving the marina, you will navigate through several moored sailboats as you head south toward Dyke Marsh Wildlife Preserve. You have a choice to either head left directly out to the deeper water of the Potomac River and then turn right around two islands, or stay along the coast and paddle in between the island and the shoreline and the adjacent Mount Vernon bike trail. If you take the latter route, you will see a wooden observation deck on the point to the right that is the end point of a spur off the Mount Vernon trail known as the Haul Road, which is a very popular area for birdwatchers.

Just past the observation deck, the route opens up, and you now have a clear view across the Potomac to Rosier Bluff on the Maryland side of the river. In the summer months, there is quite a bit of recreational boating traffic in this area, but most will be found more toward the middle of the river; the only impact being residual waves from the boats to paddle through.

Heading south and staying along the coast, you will come upon the northern portion of Dyke Marsh on the right, noticeable by the uniform level of grasses and cattails about 4 feet above water level. While we have tried several times at high tide to find an opening into the marsh here, we have been unsuccessful and have had to continue south to the major entryway about ½ mile farther. As you continue south, there will be a small island to the left that normally contains one or more osprey nests in the spring and summer months. Passing this island marks the entrance to Dyke Marsh on the right.

Winding your way through the marsh, it is important to stay in the main waterway, as detours up some of the smaller cuts can lead to difficulty in retracing your path. It is not hard at all to become disoriented paddling up one of these cuts, as it branches off to numerous other smaller waterways. You will reach the farthest point of the navigable marsh when you come upon the wooden bridge that is part of the Mount Vernon bike trail, but there is plenty of room to easily turn

Dyke Marsh

Dyke Marsh is one of the last remaining freshwater tidal marshes in the Washington, D.C., capital region and is also one of the George Washington Memorial Parkway's park sites managed by the National Park Service (NPS). The marsh got its name because it was diked (surrounded with earthen walls) in the early 1800s to protect the land from tidal influence and make more land available to graze livestock and grow crops. In the 1930s, the marsh covered an area of about 650 acres, but portions of the marsh were dredged for sand and gravel in the 1950s and 1960s. When NPS took over management in 1976, the preserve had been reduced to about 485 acres.

According to the Friends of Dyke Marsh, a volunteer group dedicated to preserving and enhancing the tidal marsh, it is estimated the marsh is eroding at the rate of about one and a half to two acres per year, and if no remedial action is taken, it will disappear in 30 to 40 years. The NPS, working with the U.S. Army Corps of Engineers, is evaluating possible options for restoration and long-term management of the preserve.

Over 200 species of birds have been observed in the Dyke Marsh Preserve; however, only about 95 species are regularly associated with the area, and of that number, about 45 have been confirmed as breeding here. In addition to the many birds that frequent the marsh, beavers, muskrat, cottontail rabbits, and snapper and painted turtles also call the wildlife preserve home.

around and head back up the marsh. Retrace your route back to the entrance of the marsh, and for a short paddle (just over 4 miles), head back toward the launch site, circumventing the islands near the marina in the reverse order of the outbound leg.

For a longer paddle (or a completely separate short paddle), continue north past the launch site and head toward the Woodrow Wilson Bridge (I-495). You will pass a couple of osprey nests on pilings, and just to the south of the bridge is a small, white building visible from the marina, the Jones Point Lighthouse. The lighthouse was built in 1855 and is the last remaining river lighthouse in the Commonwealth of Virginia.

Egret rookery in Hunting Creek

When you reach the lighthouse, turn left and paddle along the marsh grass and cattails that outline Jones Point Park. You will then

Jones Point Lighthouse

Friends paddling Hunting Creek

come to several tall apartment complexes on your right, followed by the bridge over the George Washington Memorial Parkway with its three semicircular openings that marks the entrance to Hunting Creek. Entering Hunting Creek, there will be a narrow cut 15 to 20 yards wide, which parallels the Belle Haven Country Club Golf Course. You can follow this for about ½ mile, passing under an eagle's nest. There are often birdwatchers camped adjacent to the Mount Vernon bike trail with their long telephoto lenses trained on the nest.

After exiting the cut, there are numerous other smaller paths through the spatterdock vegetation adjacent to the golf course. Also, across the creek and within a couple of hundred yards from the beltway is an egret rookery. Round-trip back to the marina for this portion of the route is about 4¾ miles.

9.

Little Hunting Creek

Directions: From Old Town Alexandria, take Washington Street
south toward Mount Vernon. Washington Street becomes the
George Washington Memorial Parkway. Go approximately 7½
miles to just past the Fort Hunt Road exit where you will see a
small parking lot on the left across from the River Farm Drive
exit, adjacent to both the Potomac River and the Mount Vernon
bike trail.

From I-495 (beltway), take US 1 south to exit 177A, staying
in the right lane. From the right lane, follow the sign for the left
turn onto Fort Hunt Road. From Fort Hunt Road, turn left on
Belle Haven Road and follow it until it ends at the George
Washington Memorial Parkway. Turn left on the parkway, and
follow the directions above to the parking lot.

GPS Coordinates: 38° 42' 36.8"; 77° 03' 27.5"

Amenities: The parking lot has space for approximately 15 cars,
and there is no launch fee and no facilities. The launch site is
at the end of the right side of the parking lot past a small picnic
table and is a combination sandy-pebbly beach at low and
midtide and small rocks at high tide. About 50 yards south
across a short wooden bridge on the bike path is a low retaining wall that is also a good put-in site at any tide. It is best to
paddle this route at or near high tide, but you can still make it a
significant way up Little Hunting Creek at any tide.

Length of Paddle: 3½–6 miles; 1½–2½ hours

Route Description

While Little Hunting Creek is probably the most residential in nature of all the tours in this book, it is also home to a wide variety of wildlife. We have encountered bald eagles, ospreys in their nests and out fishing, many herons, kingfishers, a variety of ducks (including mallards and buffleheads), cormorants, Canada geese, and turtles.

Canada geese

Paddling south paralleling the George Washington Memorial Parkway and the Mount Vernon bike trail, you will see alternating stretches along the bank of wooden and rock retaining walls. Looking south, you will see the red

Mount Vernon from the Potomac River

roofing and large oak tree on a hill that comprises Mount Vernon, about 2 miles south from your position. Combining this relatively short paddle with a tour of Mount Vernon makes for a very pleasant day in the vicinity of our nation's capital.

As you continue paddling, you will pass several stately homes along the George Washington Memorial Parkway, and then the Cedar Knoll Restaurant, an Alexandria institution that was originally owned by George Washington. The restaurant, with its commanding views of the Potomac River, is a popular location for weddings, receptions, and other events but is also a favorite spot for paddlers and bicyclers to stop for an appetizer or a beer.

About 1 mile from the put-in, you will see several trees overhanging the bank, with some that you can paddle under. Some of these trees contain the bittersweet vine with its beautiful orange and yellow berries. Like the dichotomy in its name, the vine is both a favorite for use in holiday decorations and a scourge to landscapers because of its ability to engulf other vegetation and slowly kill it.

Mount Vernon

Mount Vernon is the home and burial place of George Washington, commander in chief of the American forces in the Revolutionary War and first president of the United States. The estate was originally called Little Hunting Creek plantation and covered about 5,000 acres. George Washington's half-brother Lawrence renamed the plantation Mount Vernon in honor of Admiral Edward Vernon, whom he served with in a conflict between Great Britain and Spain in the Caribbean Sea in 1739–1742. Washington and his wife, Martha, lived in the home for more than 40 years

In 1853, Ann Pamela Cunningham of South Carolina formed the Mount Vernon Ladies' Association of the Union, which was chartered to restore and maintain the house and 200 acres of the original estate. The estate was designated a national registered historic landmark in 1960, and the Commonwealth of Virginia agreed to exempt the estate from taxation. Today, it is the most popular historic estate in America and is open every day of the year for visitors.

At this point, the bank opens up to the right, and this marks the entrance to Little Hunting Creek. You will see a white channel marker in the middle of the small bay at the entrance to the creek. As you paddle along the bank, it will appear there is no opening, but you will soon come to the concrete bridge spanning the parkway. Paddling under the bridge, the creek opens up to a wide expanse of undeveloped marsh and forest on the left side and residential housing with docks

Bittersweet berries

and boats along the right bank. At any times other than slack tide (about one hour either side of high or low tide), there will be a 2- to 4-knot current that, because of the very narrow opening under the bridge, can cause some swirling water conditions. Once clear of the bridge, the marsh area will continue for approximately ¾ mile before you encounter the first houses along the left bank. Staying along the left bank for this stretch will provide the best opportunity for seeing the various birds and other wildlife you may encounter.

As you continue up the creek, you will alternate between stretches of a few houses with their accompanying boat docks on one side of the creek and areas of uninhabited marsh grass that contain both beautiful flora, as well as the birds and animals previously mentioned.

While the creek overall is mostly navigable by kayaks, in low and midtide, you will encounter shallow areas on either side of the creek. There are red and green channel markers along the length of the creek, and if you stay near either side of the markers, you should have plenty of water to paddle up to the farthest reaches of the creek.

After a 90-degree bend to the right, the creek narrows down to about 30 yards across, roughly maintaining this width for two more

Exiting Little Hunting Creek

slight bends, before you come to an area where the creek opens up a bit and there is a fork (in about ⅔ mile); you can paddle either to the left along the few remaining houses and docks or over to the right, where there are no noticeable dwellings. Both routes can be paddled for about another 700 yards and offer the chance to see additional wildlife.

Once you have either chosen a direction, or decided to paddle both, retrace your route and return back to the launch point. To extend the paddle, once you exit Little Hunting Creek, stay right and circumvent the small bay that is devoid of human habitation and is another very good area for wildlife spotting. This will add about 1 mile to your route.

10.

Occoquan River: Occoquan Regional Park

Directions: From the I-495 (beltway), take I-95 south to exit 160, VA 123 (Gordon Boulevard). Continue on VA 123 north for four stoplights, and then take a right into Occoquan Regional Park.

GPS Coordinates: 38° 40' 48" N; 77° 15' 21" W

Amenities: The launch area accommodates all sizes of boats, and there is a large parking area for boat/trailer combos and cars as well. There are soda/water vending and ice machines in close proximity, and the launch fee is $4 per kayak: if an attendant is not there, put the money in an envelope next to the ramp. Kayak rentals and instruction are available as well. For more information, see www.nvrpa.org/park/occoquan.

As you enter the park, there is a small parking lot on the left side for those who want to take in a scenic view that looks out over the historic town of Occoquan on the other side of the Occoquan River. It's a 30- to 40-minute round-trip hike with a steep incline at the start for about 50 yards, but relatively flat after that. In addition to the boat launch facilities, the park contains athletic fields, batting cages, picnic tables near the river, and fishing spots where anglers can fish for largemouth bass, carp, crappie, catfish, striped bass, and perch.

The park is also part of the Potomac Heritage National Scenic Trail and the Occoquan Water Trail. The Potomac Heritage Trail is a network of hiking, bicycling, paddling, and driving routes that follow the paths explored by George Washington throughout Virginia, Washington, D.C., Maryland, and Pennsylvania. The Occoquan Water Trail, described in more detail in chapter 12, is a 40-mile route on two tributaries of the Chesapeake Bay.

Length of Paddle: 4½–7 miles; 2–3 hours

Route Description

Departing from the boat ramp, you can turn right and take a short paddle under the US 123 bridge to the historic town of Occoquan on the southern bank of the river. There are several nice restaurants and taverns both along the river and within a short walking distance from where you can tie up. The lower Occoquan Dam is another 100 yards upriver from the town and marks the turnaround point for the first part of the route.

Heading back downriver under the US 123 bridge and past the put-in point, you will pass several marinas on the right (southern) bank and on the left—and much more interesting—the more unspoiled Occoquan Park land, with a few small boat ramps and picnic gazebos overlooking the water.

During the spring and summer months, there will be a large amount of recreational boat traffic navigating up and down the river, so staying along the northern bank is both safer and more interesting. Stands of pickerelweed, cattails, honeysuckle vine, and daylilies are all present along the shoreline, and just before the first bridge is a large cove completely filled with spatterdock vegetation (also called cow lily). You will then paddle in between huge pylons that support the two massive bridges of I-95 southbound and northbound, carrying the majority of car and truck traffic from Boston and points north, down to the southern portion of Florida (Miami).

The next bridge you come to will be the US 1 (Jefferson Davis Highway) bridge, and while you would expect this area to be clogged with waterfront housing, it is surprisingly devoid of development. There are very steep rises of rock and vegetation that are quite interesting when paddling close by. Gnarly evergreens extending down to

The Occoquan Workhouse

As you make your way from the park entrance to the launch site, take note of the historic Occoquan Workhouse and the accompanying commemorative marker. The workhouse pays tribute to the American women's rights movement, which began in 1848 at the Seneca Falls Convention in New York. There, with the help of the former slave and famous abolitionist Frederick Douglass, a resolution was passed: "Resolved, which is the duty of women of this country to secure to themselves their sacred right to the elective franchise." Progress for the women's suffrage movement was slow for many decades after, and even though an amendment to the Constitution was first proposed by Susan B. Anthony and Elizabeth Cady Stanton in 1878, it wasn't until the National Woman's Party was formed in 1916 that the federal government began to take notice.

Members of the Woman's Party began picketing the White House, and in June of 1917, many were arrested for unlawful assembly and sentenced either to pay a $25 fine or serve a jail term. The women preferred jail time to paying the fine. One of the jails they were confined to was the Lorton Reformatory in nearby Lorton, Virginia (converted to the Lorton Workhouse Arts Center in 2008). In 1920, the 19th amendment to the Constitution was passed, prohibiting any U.S. citizen the right to vote based on sex. The women prisoners of Occoquan played a significant role in the amendment's passage.

Historic Occoquan Workhouse

Occoquan River barge loading station

the water's surface are intermixed with wild roses, trumpet creeper, and daylilies.

On the southern bank, you will see a huge industrial complex, the Occoquan River Barge Loading Station. During working hours, you can watch the very deliberate and massive operation of taking the raw sand material from the barges that are brought up the river, dumping it into a huge hopper, and transporting it several hundred yards on conveyor belts up to the processing plant.

The next and final bridge you will encounter will be a railroad bridge that carries both commuter and commercial transport trains. During a typical paddle, you will most likely see either type of train heading north or south; on our most recent paddle, we saw a CSX transport train with 4 engines and 80 cars go over the bridge.

Paddling under the railroad bridge, on the left (north) bank, you will see the private Captain John S. Beach Marina, followed by another pristine stretch that includes the ever-present (in spring through fall months) spatterdock vegetation. There is a grounded barge about 100 yards from shore, and from this point on, there is a wide variety of wildlife along the shoreline and in the water. We have seen bald eagles, great blue herons, egrets, and flocks of geese and coots on our paddles here.

After passing another marina, you will approach the entrance to Massey Creek, where several very large houses on the shoreline mark the entrance to the creek. If you choose to turn around at this point, returning to the boat ramp would be about a 4½-mile paddle.

To extend your route, head up the creek where the deep-water channel is to the left, adjacent to the houses and their associated docks. You can paddle outside the channel and over to the right bank, though, where you will encounter more spatterdock and an occasional beaver lodge. You can follow the creek about 1¼ miles before having to turn around.

Exiting Massey Creek and returning upriver, you may encounter several different flocks of birds including pied-billed grebes (also called hell-divers and water witches), goldeneye and bufflehead ducks, and a line of over 500 coots stretched over several hundred yards. While most of the duck families we encounter on the water are extremely skittish, making it difficult to paddle close to them, the coots are a different story, and you can get very close before they all fly away. The sight and sound of several hundred coots taking flight from the water is a special event, likened to the rain from a thunderstorm on the water, as the birds' wings tap-tap the surface before becoming airborne.

The bufflehead and goldeneye ducks are migratory, diving ducks, and it is very rare that you can get within 40 or 50 yards of

Bufflehead duck

them before they either dive or take off to another location. The bufflehead is one of the smallest of the American ducks, and its name comes from their uniquely shaped bulbous heads (similar to a buffalo's). The goldeneye, also known as the common goldeneye, is slightly larger than the

Goldeneye duck

bufflehead with a distinctive golden-yellow eye, and the males have a small white circular patch under their eyes.

Paddling to the end of Massey Creek and retracing your route back to the launch site is about a 7-mile paddle.

11.

Occoquan Reservoir

THE 2,100-ACRE Occoquan Reservoir is one of the premier recreational destinations for water activities in Northern Virginia. Over 15 miles in length, it is home to four county and regional parks (three are described here), and is considered to be one of the best fisheries in the state. The reservoir is formed by the Upper Occoquan Dam, completed in 1957, and it delineates the border between Prince William and Fairfax Counties.

Lake Ridge Park and Marina

Directions: From I-495 (beltway), take I-95 south to exit 160B at the town of Occoquan. Take VA 123 north (Gordon Boulevard). Continue north on VA 123 to second crossroad, VA 641 west (Old Bridge Road). Turn left on VA 641. Continue 3½ miles to Hodges Run Drive, and turn right. Go 1/5 mile, turn left on Cotton Mill Drive, and follow it to Lake Ridge Park entrance; the road dead-ends at the marina. There is an alternate launch site and paddle description at the end of this chapter.

GPS Coordinates: 38° 41' 50" N, 77° 19' 05" W

Amenities: During the spring through fall season, there is a snack bar and restrooms at the marina, but these facilities are closed for the winter, November through March. Kayaks can be rented for $9 an hour and $32 all day. There is a $3 launch fee for kayaks payable at the marina or, when the marina concession is closed, at the Golf Course Pro shop up the hill.

Length of Paddle: 3½–9 miles; 1½–4 hours

Route Description

This particular launch site is also home to several high school rowing crews, Woodbridge, Potomac, Garfield, CD Hylton, and Forest Park. The marina has a large boat ramp separate from the rowing crew's ramps, and after launching from the boat ramp, head right toward the open water of the Occoquan Reservoir.

When you approach the reservoir proper, on the far bank, you will see number marker 5. These are GPS markers along the entire length of the reservoir, and serve to provide rowers and other boaters with location markers for emergency situations.

Turn right, down the reservoir, toward the Occoquan Dam. Along the southern (right) bank, you will see several large houses followed by apartment and townhouse complexes. The far (left) bank is much more pristine, with no dwellings and only walking paths along the shore.

Continuing down the reservoir, on the right shore, you will see several rock outcrops painted bright colors with high school rowing emblems and other graffiti. As you continue on, there are several cuts on both sides of the reservoir, most fairly short, but some worth explor-

Lake Ridge Park launch ramp

ing, as wildlife tends to favor these more isolated areas. On our most recent paddle, we spotted a bald eagle flying and then landing on an upper tree branch. Shortly thereafter, a red-tailed hawk flew over and accosted the eagle, and we realized the hawk was after what the eagle had already killed for its meal.

After GPS marker 3, you will come to the Sandy Run Regional Park on the left point where heading left of the park will take you up an isolated inlet you can follow a little more than 1 mile,

Great blue heron

and heading right, you will continue down the reservoir toward the dam. The park has facilities for competitive and recreational rowing that are used by high schools, colleges, and some national organizations. There is no public boat launch access here, and the park is open to the public only on days of rowing regattas.

After passing the regional park, you will come upon several cascading benches and then a set of bleachers along the shoreline that represent the finish line of the high school crew race courses.

As mentioned, the left shore is more isolated; however, there are walking/jogging paths along both banks. Along the left shore, you will encounter several interesting rock outcrops that come right down to the water's edge.

After GPS marker 2, you will come along an historic marker on a small island off the left shoreline. The marker commemorates a significant Confederate advance during the Civil War at Selecman's Ford, a narrow river crossing near here that was flooded when the Occoquan Dam was built in 1958.

Between GPS markers 2 and 1, you will paddle under two sets of massive power lines that help feed the nearly insatiable electrical demand of the Northern Virginia–Washington, D.C., megalopolis. This marks both the turnaround point of the paddle as you see the line of orange buoys across the reservoir delineating the Occoquan Dam and power station, as well as the start of the rowing crew race course. For those that want to extend the paddle, there is a relatively large inlet off to the right of the dam barrier that continues for another 1 mile before it gets too shallow to paddle.

On returning back to the launch site, you obviously have the option of paddling along either bank, or down the middle of the reservoir. We prefer to paddle along one shoreline because of the greater opportunity to observe wildlife. On our most recent paddle, we decided to make the return trip along the opposite bank, the one with all of the housing. To our surprise, we spotted a deer lying down on the bank, with another one nearby. Paddling to the orange buoys, and returning to the launch site is about a 6-mile route, and continuing up the inlet to the right adds another 2 miles.

A deer on the banks of the Occoquan Reservoir

Fountainhead Regional Park

Directions: Follow the directions above to VA 123 (Gordon Boulevard) at Occoquan. Head north on VA 123 approximately 5
miles. Turn left onto Hampton Road, and drive 3 miles to the
entrance of Fountainhead Regional Park on the left.

GPS Coordinates: 38° 43' 15" N; 77° 20' 03" W

Amenities: Fountainhead Regional Park is open daily March 20
through November 13, from dawn to dusk. It is closed November 14 for the winter. There are restroom facilities in the marina
shop, and there is a $2 launch fee for kayaks.

   Additional amenities include guided kayak tours, mountain
bike and nature trails, and access to the 17-mile Bull Run–
Occoquan Trail (no bikes). The park rents kayaks ($9.50/hour),
canoes, johnboats, and electric motorboats. More information
can be found at www.nvrpa.org/park/fountainhead.

Length of Paddle: 3–6 miles; 1½–3 hours

Route Description

Similar to paddling from Lake Ridge Park Marina, you have a choice of
paddling up or down the reservoir; again, wind is one of the main factors to take into account in deciding which way to go. Another very nice
aspect of paddling the reservoir is there is a 10 hp limit on boat motors,
which significantly reduces both the noise and wave impact on the
reservoir. This obviously makes for more wildlife present in the vicinity, and we have observed herons, ducks, and geese, as well as eagles and
ospreys diving and retrieving fish.

   Heading up the reservoir (to the right), there is an isolated inlet just
to the right that you can paddle up about ⅓ mile before having to turn
around. This portion of the reservoir is slightly wider than farther
down, so the current (what little there is) is slower here.

   Passing GPS marker 12 and approaching marker 13, there is a series
of abandoned marina pilings on the left bank. Just across this on the
right bank is another inlet that can be paddled for about ⅓ mile. From
this point, in about another ½ mile, the reservoir makes a very sharp

bend to the left. Paddling up both inlets mentioned here and to the bend and returning is about a 4-mile round-trip.

To paddle down the reservoir, head left from the landing, and just past GPS marker 11 on the left is a nice inlet to explore. Occasionally you will see rowing crews from the Lake Ridge Marina boathouse in both four- and eight-man shells practicing, with their coaches in johnboats alongside giving instruction. Also along the left shore are multiple places to either rest or have a picnic lunch.

At GPS marker 8, there are interesting rock outcrops along the shore, and as you approach GPS marker 6, you will encounter the first of several housing developments along this stretch on the right bluff. From the launch site to marker 6 (and exploring the inlet) and back is about a 4¼-mile paddle, so you can either return at this point or continue down the reservoir.

12.

Occoquan Reservoir: Bull Run Marina

Directions: From I-495 (beltway), take I-66 west to exit 55A, MD 7100 south (Fairfax County Parkway). Continue on the parkway to VA 123 (West Ox Road), and turn right. At Clifton Road, turn right, and then left on Henderson Road for 3 miles to a right turn on Old Yates Ford Road. The marina entrance is 7/10 mile to a dirt road on the right, just before the bridge that crosses over Bull Run.

GPS Coordinates: 38° 44' 33" N; 77° 23' 15" W

Amenities: This site doubles as a starting point for several high school rowing crews with storage areas for their rowing shells. There is ample parking 50 yards uphill from the launch site and restroom facilities adjacent to the parking lot.

While this particular paddle is one of the finest narrow-waterway routes in the book, it does require an annual membership fee through the Northern Virginia Parks and Recreation Association, as described in the introduction, and in addition, you will need to purchase a key for $15, which gives you specific access for one year to the Bull Run Marina launch. The annual pass and key can be purchased at Fountainhead Regional Park a few miles downstream and described in the Occoquan Reservoir: Lake Ridge Park and Marina section.

This paddle is also part of the Occoquan Water Trail, a 40-mile route on two tributaries of the Chesapeake Bay. The upper segment covers Bull Run to the Occoquan Reservoir, and the lower segment covers Pohick and Accotink bays and Gunston

Cove. There are eight launch sites along the trail, and five are starting points in this book. More information on the trail can be found at www.nvrpa.org/park/occoquan_water_trail. Also associated with the trail is the Occoquan Watertrail League (OWL), a group of paddlers and other volunteers who work with local governments and landowners to maintain and improve access to the water trail and promote resource and environmental awareness. More information on the league can be found at http://owlva.org/cms/Trail_Map_files.

Length of Paddle: 4–9 miles; 1½–4 hours

Route Description

The launch point consists of a concrete ramp for launching boats flanked on both sides by very shallow floating docks perfect for launching kayaks and other small watercraft. This marks the farthest point upstream for the rowing crews, so they will all be heading downstream toward the Occoquan Reservoir from this point.

Departing from the docks, on your left and downstream about 20 yards is the bridge that crosses over Bull Run, Old Yates Ford Road. Turn right and head upstream, paddling in between several old bridge

Bull Run Marina launch site

Bull Run in the Civil War

Bull Run was the site of two of the most infamous battles in Civil War History, the first, also known as First Manassas (the name used by the Confederate forces), was fought on July 21, 1862. This was the first major land battle fought in the Civil War, and where then Colonel Thomas Jackson received his nickname "Stonewall," when his confederate troops stood their ground (temporarily) against a much larger number of Union forces until reinforcements from the Shenandoah Valley turned the tide and drove the Yankees into retreat.

The Second Battle of Bull Run or Second Manassas was fought August 28–30, 1862, on the same ground as First Manassas. It was considered to be one of the most significant victories by the Confederate army in the war.

This was a much larger battle, pitting 55,000 Confederate soldiers under General Robert E. Lee's Army against the 75,000 Union forces under Major General John Pope. As General Pope's troops waited for General McClellan's Army of the Potomac to arrive for a combined offensive, General Lee struck first by sending half of his army (under Colonel Jackson), to attack the Federal supply base at Manassas. They seized the depot's supplies and burned it to the ground, and then hid in the woods. On 29 August, the two armies clashed, and there were heavy losses on both sides.

The next day, the remaining 28,000 troops of General Lee's army arrived and launched a counterattack, forcing General Pope to withdraw his army back toward Washington. There were over 14,000 Union soldier casualties (dead wounded and missing), and over 9,000 Confederate soldier casualties. General Lee continued to press his advantage, crossing the Potomac into Maryland. General McClellan united his army with the Army of Virginia, marched to the northwest and confronted General Lee's army at Antietam. On September 17, the two armies clashed in the Battle of Antietam, the single deadliest war in American history.

abutments. You will immediately encounter one of several small islands on this route, and you can paddle on either side of each of them.

After launching one day, we immediately noticed a red-tailed hawk screeching and soaring overhead, and this was repeated probably

Tree stumps in Bull Run

another 10 times by other hawks and raptors throughout the paddle. Along the left bank, you will notice several stately houses perched on a short, steep hillside, but these quickly give way to almost no other dwellings for the rest of the paddle.

The creek is about 60 yards wide at this point, and in another ¼ mile, it opens up to a much broader expanse as you turn left around the first bend. On the right bank, there will be an open field, and then the first of many tree stump "farms," a series of several hundred fully and partially submerged stumps in the shallow water. While it is fun to paddle through these areas, a word of caution; go slow, because there is nothing more discon-

Virginia Bluebell

certing than paddling onto a stump and having difficulty getting yourself dislodged (or worse, tipping over!).

Continuing up-creek, there are a few more islands that you can paddle on either side of, some with evidence of beavers and their lodge-building activities. The creek necks down at this point to about 30 yards across, and with no dwellings on either side,

Viburnum in flower

the wildlife is varied and plentiful, including bald eagles, herons, ospreys, territorial kingfishers, trilling red-bellied woodpeckers, and turtles. River birches and other trees angle across the center of the creek from the shoreline and in some places the branches form a canopy overhead. There are also several wildflowers that grow very close to the banks, including Virginia bluebell and viburnum.

You will likely encounter folks fishing in small johnboats in these stretches, but with only electric motors allowed, there is little man-made noise with one exception: the Fairfax Rod and Gun Club. The club's shooting range is nearby, and when the range is open, there is a fairly continuous cacophony of guns firing.

After traversing a few more bends in the creek, you will come upon a small tributary on the left, adjacent to a dirt road that comes down to the water's edge, and a picnic table on the bank. Turning around here makes for a round-trip 5-mile paddle, but there are several more miles of navigable water if you want to extend your route.

A second way to extend your route is to return past the launch site and head under the Old Yates Ford Road Bridge. This is where the effects of the Occoquan Dam are first evident as the waterway opens to between 100 and 200 yards across. This stretch slowly bends around to the right, and you will come to a fork in about 1½ miles. Staying to the right takes you down the main portion of the reservoir, and the fork to the left is the entrance to the Occoquan River. You can follow this tributary for several miles as it necks down to about 80 yards across after a big bend to the left, and a good distance marker is the Davis Ford Road Bridge about 2 miles from the fork.

13.

Aquia Creek:
Willow Landing Marina

Directions: Take I-95 south to exit 140A, Courthouse Road, and head east to US 1 (Richmond Highway). Turn left on US 1, and then right on Hope Road. Go approximately 3 miles where you will see the sign for Willow Landing Marina.

An alternate put-in site is Hope Springs Marina. Continue on Hope Road past Willow Landing Marina approximately 1½ miles to Hope Springs.

GPS Coordinates: Willow Marina Landing—77° 22' 03" N; 38° 25' 51" W;

Hope Springs Marina—38° 25' 20" N; 77° 21' 31" W

Amenities: Willow Landing Marina has a small convenience store with soda and ice machines and restroom facilities. Launch fees are $15 per car, using the honor system (place envelope in lockbox) in the off-season. Hope Springs Marina is a large boating facility that has ample parking, a convenience store, restroom facilities in-season, and a portable toilet off-season. Launch fees are $20 per vehicle. Launch from here if you want a longer route that includes an extra 2 miles of additional open-water paddling.

Length of Paddle: 5–8 miles; 2¼–3½ hours

Route Description

The launch site at Willow Landing Marina is a narrow, shallow concrete boat ramp with docks on both sides. Once you clear the boat slip area, head slightly left across the wide portion of Aquia Creek, with marsh grass all along the left bank, before you reach the narrower portion of the creek, marked by the green channel marker 25.

On our most recent paddle, we encountered several large flocks of coots in these open waters, a good harbinger of the wildlife we would observe on the rest of the paddle. Several species of ducks also call these waters home, as evidenced by the multiple duck blinds encircling this open stretch of the creek.

While initially you will find the marsh grass on the left (with a solitary tree jutting out here and there) and huge houses on hills on the right bank, throughout the remainder of the route, the undeveloped, nearly ever-present marsh grass will alternate with both expansive houses with massive docks and much smaller houses and trailers along the shorelines.

Willow Landing put-in on Aquia Creek

When you get to channel marker 25A, the creek bends to the left, and there are walking trails along the right bank. This is the part of the creek where the amount and diversity of the wildlife significantly increases. We have seen several species of ducks, eagles, and red-tailed and Cooper's hawks soaring overhead, and egrets and great blue herons fishing and gliding between fishing spots.

Cooper's hawk

Rounding the next bend to the right, and adjacent to red channel marker 28, you will see an open field on the left with a small boat ramp and picnic area. While the boat ramp is private, you are allowed to pull up your kayak either for a rest or to use it as a nice spot to stop for a lunch or a snack.

In about another ¼ mile, the creek narrows down significantly, with the aforementioned smaller houses and trailers along the left bank and marshland with many more trees along the right. These trees are magnets for many types of birds, including hawks, kingfishers, chickadees, woodpeckers, and red-winged blackbirds. We have also observed a herd of six deer frolicking along the bank just past this stretch of houses.

The creek bends again to the left here after passing green channel marker 33, with some of the largest houses on the creek perched on the hillside on the right bank. There are more walking trails along the left, which is part of Government Island Park, a truly unique national asset with a rich historic tradition and a designated site on the Potomac Heritage National Scenic Trail. The park is one of the few areas where, in addition to a variety of birds and aquatic flowers and vegetation, we have seen muskrats up close chewing on spatterdock flowers and transporting other grasses to their nests.

Government Island Park

In 1694, George Brent established a quarry at this location (then known as Wigginton's Island), because it was a major source of Aquia Creek sandstone. The building material was used in many government buildings in Washington, D.C., including the White House and the U.S. Capitol. The quarry was purchased on behalf of the U.S. government by Pierre Charles L'Enfant in 1791 and was then named Government Island.

Over time, it was discovered the sandstone was more susceptible to weathering than other building materials and use of the stone significantly declined into the early 19th century. The government sold the island in 1963 to Stafford County, and it is now a natural park preserve and archaeological site. The park contains 1½ miles of walking trails with several historical markers. If you have the time, a visit here is well worth a detour.

To get to the park, follow the directions above, then take Hope Road back to US 1 and turn right onto US 1 north. Go about 1½ miles, and turn right on Coal Landing Road. Follow Coal Landing Road about ½ mile to the park trailhead on the left. The trail is open daily: mid-March to October, 8 AM–8 PM; November to mid-March, 8 AM–5:30 PM.

Government Island quarry stone

Muskrat in spatterdock vegetation

Turning around at this point would make for a 5-mile round-trip paddle; however, you can continue another ½ mile, passing the rest of Government Island to the left until the creek forks. This marks the beginning of a small, uninhabited island that can be circumnavigated by paddling another 1¾ miles. Heading to the left, you will shortly come upon the private Aquia Harbour Yacht Club and another fork, so stay right to continue around the island. By continuing to stay right when you encounter another two forks in the creek, you will successfully make your way around the island along this 30-to-40-yard-wide portion of the creek, before returning to the launch site.

14.

Abel Reservoir

Directions: From I-495 (beltway), take I-95 south to exit 140,
Courthouse Road. Take Courthouse Road west (right turn);
continue 2 miles to just past Colonial Forge High School on the
left, and turn left on Ramoth Church Road. Travel 1½ miles to
Kellogg Mill Road, and turn right. Continue on Kellogg Mill Road
2 miles, over the bridge for the Abel Reservoir; take the next
right into the put-in site for the reservoir.

GPS Coordinates: 38° 24' 51" N, 77° 29' 46" W

Amenities: The put-in site is a dirt and gravel parking area for
about 10 cars with no facilities and no launch fee. While there
is neither a ramp nor a dock, the launch area is very straightforward, with a shallow slope and soft sand and gravel base for
an easy launch and recovery.

Length of Paddle: 4–7 miles; 1¾–3 hours

Route Description

This is another great route for the beginner or intermediate paddler
who wants to practice their paddling technique. The reservoir is a beautiful, sinuous, 185-acre waterway that at most times is perfectly calm
but can become slightly choppy with some wind. The reservoir provides drinking water for Stafford County, and it is primarily used by
fishermen seeking out the abundance of bass, crappie, chain pickerel,
bluegill, and catfish. If you are at all interested in kayak fishing, this is
a prime location because of its many weedy spots and inlets, as well as
its relative isolation compared to other waterways in the area.

Abel Reservoir put-in site

Leaving the launch site, head right and proceed under the sloping Kellogg Mill Road Bridge. For the first ¼ mile, there are a handful of houses on the hillside along the right shore, but during the late spring and summer months, they are all nearly obscured by the foliage. For the next mile or so, there are no houses on either side, and the tranquility is even more assured than most sites around Washington, D.C., because there are no gasoline engines allowed on the reservoir. About the only noise you will hear are the small planes landing and taking off from nearby Stafford Regional Airport, about 1 mile from the closest point of the reservoir. The reservoir widens out slightly at this point, giving way to steep-sided banks on both sides, and there are several interesting rock-face outcrops along the left shore.

The wildlife we have observed here belies the relatively small size of the basin. On our most recent paddle one December, we saw three red-tailed hawks (one of which circled above us at about 50 feet for over a minute; the other two following each other from tree to tree), an eagle soaring overhead, a gaggle of over 100 geese, several diving ducks, cormorants, and a beaver lodge. Combining this with, on occasion,

Rock outcrops

encountering no other craft on the water makes this one of the premier paddles within an hour of D.C.

Regarding red-tailed hawks, they are the most common hawks in North America, with five different subspecies in the United States (and not all have red tails!). These beautiful, relatively large raptors prefer open areas, yet they have adapted to almost every environment, including mountains and even urban settings. You can frequently observe them on the tops of telephone or power poles along the highway and on the corners of tall buildings. While red-tailed hawks eat mostly small birds and mammals (mice, voles, rabbits, and squirrels), they are frequently spotted soaring over and in the vicinity of waterways. We have observed them on nearly every paddling route in this book. Their abundance coupled with the fact they are relatively easily trained make them the most

Soaring red-tailed hawk

popular choice of raptor for falconry. Their unique screech is often used as the definitive raptor sound in television shows and movies.

As you continue winding your way down the reservoir, take note of the large stands of hemlocks, as well as the high-water mark of the reservoir, noticeable by the discoloration of the foliage along the banks. The eastern hemlock (also known as the Canada hemlock) is a slow-growing conifer tree that may take up to 300 years to reach maturity and may live for 800 years or more! Unfortunately, both types of hemlock are under attack by the hemlock woolly adelgid, a small aphidlike insect that has decimated strands up and down the eastern United States.

Continuing up the reservoir, you will eventually come to the terminus marked by a large earthen dam on the left. For the shortest route, reverse course here and return to the launch site. To extend your paddle, there are several interesting small cuts to explore, two of which are adjacent to the earthen dam, and others can be accessed on the return route. In the wintertime, some of these cuts may contain a thin layer of ice.

Potomac Run creek entering the reservoir

Once back at the launch site, you can continue past it for about another ⅓ mile up Potomac Creek before you reach some small ripples that mark the turnaround point. The creek is a 17-mile-long tributary of the Potomac River and empties into the Potomac River at Marlboro Point, just south of Aquia Creek. There are also several small stone walls along the shoreline here, as well as a walking path that parallels the creek and is accessible from the launch point.

15.
Pohick Bay: Pohick Bay Regional Park

Directions: From I-495 (beltway), take I-95 south to exit 161 to
Lorton, US 1 north. Go about 1½ miles to the first stoplight and
turn right on Gunston Road. Go about 4 miles to Pohick Bay
Regional Park; entrance is on the left.

GPS Coordinates: 38° 40' 37" N; 77° 10' 07" W

Amenities: The park is open seven days a week, 7 AM–dark;
there is a $4 launch fee for residents of Arlington, Fairfax,
and Loudoun counties and the cities of Alexandria, Fairfax,
and Falls Church and a $6 launch fee for nonresidents. There
are restroom facilities adjacent to the parking lot. Kayak rentals
and instruction are available as well. Kayaks can be rented for
$8.50 an hour or $37 a day for residents; $9.50 an hour and
$41 a day for nonresidents. The park also has guided canoe
and kayak trips, camping, miniature golf, and a Frisbee disc
golf course on site. For more information, see www.nvrpa
.org/parks/pohickbay/index.php.

Length of Paddle: 3½–5¾ miles; 1¾–2¾ hours

Route Description

Entering the boat launch area, there are two boat ramps to the right of
a very large parking lot. While you can launch here, at the far end of the
parking lot is a terrific sandy beach that is the preferred spot for launching car-top watercraft.

This has become one of our favorite paddles because of the large diversity in wildlife seen on each trip, as well as the crystal-clear water in Pohick Bay. While it's not required to go at or near high tide, the higher water levels allow you to paddle farther up both Pohick and Accotink Creeks.

Once you launch, turn left and follow the shoreline. You will see a few houses along this portion of the paddle, but these will be the only ones visible along the route. During the spring through fall months, you will encounter underwater grass beds and spatterdock vegetation (also called cow lily) covering the surface of a significant portion of Pohick Bay. After about ¼ mile, you will see large stands of spatterdock and the entrance to Pohick Creek. In areas free of the grass beds, you will be able to see in excess of 6 feet to the bottom. We have spotted 12-inch to 18-inch catfish, slightly smaller bass, and turtles swimming near our boats.

On our most recent paddle, on New Year's Day, in unseasonably warm mid-50-degree weather, most of the Potomac River upstream of Pohick Bay was iced in at the launch points, but the majority of Pohick Bay was ice free. Ice did fill in portions of the Pohick and Accotink Creeks, but we still were able to get in an hour and a half paddle and saw over 30 great blue herons, several eagles, and a variety of ducks—goldeneyes, buffleheads, and mallards.

Upon entering Pohick Creek, the spatterdock will guide your way in the spring through fall months. It is recommended to stay in the main channel on the way up the creek and save any exploring of side channels, of which there are several, for the way back. As you head up the creek, depending on the season, there are beautiful, white marsh mallow flowers (used for both medicinal and ornamental purposes) and purple pickerelweed flowers along the banks. You

Marsh mallow in flower

Wooden bridge on Pohick Creek

may encounter some bass fishermen, even quite a ways up-creek as you continue on.

After exploring the creek for about 1¼ miles, you will pass under a wooden walking bridge and, shortly after that, a point where the creek shallows to small ripples over the bottom. On our last paddle as we reached this turnaround point, we saw an adult deer crossing the creek about 50 yards farther than our position. Traveling back down the creek, there is a cut to the right that you can follow all the way back to Pohick Bay. About halfway along the cut, we encountered an egret rookery with about 30 adult and immature egrets vying for vantage points on two dead trees.

Once you have exited the creek and reentered Pohick Bay, stay left and paddle along the shore as the bay curves around. There's an abundance of herons and egrets to be found along the shoreline. About ½ mile up the cove, the shoreline opens up considerably, marking the entrance to Accotink Creek. For a shorter paddle (about 3½ miles), head back across Pohick Bay to the launch point, passing a small island in the middle of the bay.

For the longer paddle, turn left into one of two entrances of Accotink Creek. In the spring through fall months, you will encounter lots of spatterdock vegetation similar to the Pohick Creek entrance. Staying to the left, you may come across a heron rookery in the trees along the shore. We have also observed upward of 30 herons along this stretch. Like Pohick Creek, you can paddle about 1 mile up the creek before having to turn around because of the shallow depth.

On the return trip back to Pohick Bay, when you reach a fork in the creek, stay left to paddle a new stretch of the creek. After exiting Accotink Creek, head across Pohick Bay back to the launch point.

16.
Belmont Bay/Kanes Creek: Mason Neck State Park

Directions: From I-495 (beltway), take I-95 south to exit 161 to Lorton, US 1 north. Go about 1½ miles to the first stoplight and turn right on Gunston Road. Go about 5 miles to the Mason Neck State Park; entrance is on the right.

GPS Coordinates: 38° 38' 40" N; 77° 11' 57" W

Amenities/History: Mason Neck State Park, open every day, 8 AM–dusk, has a $4 entrance fee per vehicle and no launch fee. The park covers over 1,800 acres and has hiking, biking and self-guided trails, a large picnic area and playground, and kayaks, canoes, and bicycles for rent from April through October. The park's visitors center has a beautiful view of Belmont Bay and includes a gift shop, some snacks, and restrooms near the launch site. Additional information about the park can be found at www.dcr.virginia.gov/state_parks/mas.shtml.

Mason Neck is named after George Mason, the author of the Virginia Declaration of Rights, and the recorded history of the area began around 1755 with the construction of his plantation home, nearby Gunston Hall (now a national historic landmark owned by the Commonwealth of Virginia). The land was home to the Dogue Indian tribe before being settled by Europeans in the 1600s.

During the 19th and early 20th centuries, much of the land was used for logging of mature pine and hardwood timber. The logging, combined with the increasing pollution brought about by the influx of more and more people into Northern Virginia, caused a significant decline in the number of bald eagles in the region. By the 1960s, however, much of the forest had grown back, and in 1969, the Elizabeth Hartwell Mason Neck National Wildlife Refuge was established by the U.S. Fish and Wildlife Service. This 2,200-acre parcel of land contains the largest freshwater marsh in Northern Virginia, and it was the first federal refuge developed to protect the nesting, feeding, and roosting habitat of the (then) endangered bald eagle.

The refuge is also part of the Mason Neck Management Area, a cooperative arrangement between Mason Neck State and Pohick Bay Regional Parks, Gunston Hall Plantation, and the Bureau of Land Management's Meadowood Farm, which protects more than 6,000 acres of the Mason Neck Peninsula. In addition to the protection still afforded to the bald eagle, it is also home to one of the largest heron rookeries on the East Coast, with over 1,400 nests. It's hard to paddle more than a few hundred yards here without seeing one or the other of these grand, graceful species thriving in their natural habitat.

Length of Paddle: 3½–8 miles; 1¾–3½ hours

Route Description

The car-top launch site is at the bottom of a sloping drive, and there is parking adjacent to the visitors center, about 100 yards up from the sandy beach put-in. Departing from the launch site, head right up Belmont Bay and toward Kanes Creek, passing the visitors center on the right bank. Along this stretch of parkland are walking paths and observation points atop slowly eroding dirt cliffs, with whole trees deposited in the bay, as well as spots for bank fishing. You will shortly come upon the skeleton of a wooden boat wreck with swamp iris growing among its beams, and then the first of many duck blinds dotting the bay.

While you can make it all the way up Kanes Creek at just about any tide, it's best to paddle closer to high tide to avoid some of the shallow stretches that can make traversing the creek more difficult. During the spring through fall months, the spatterdock and pickerelweed stands occupy a significant portion of the upper bay and Kanes Creek. The two can be distinguished by the size and shape of their leaves (pickerelweed

Mason Neck launch site

being much narrower) and their flowers—those of the spatterdock are small, yellow globes while pickerelweed flowers are long, thin, and purple. You will see these almost the entire length of the creek, and they offer the opportunity to paddle in and out of the smaller stands as you approach the narrower Kanes Creek proper.

Belmont Bay and the Kanes Creek watershed is one of the premier bald eagle sites along the Potomac River, with ospreys and other rap-

tors equally prevalent, soaring overhead and alighting in trees along the banks. This abundance of wildlife combined with the number and variety of game fish inhabiting the creek and bay make this one of the most popular spots for recreational paddlers and anglers alike. Add to that the isolation afforded by protected parkland on both sides

Pickerelweed in flower

Great blue heron in flight

of the creek, and you have one of the premier paddling spots in the region.

The entrance to the creek will be framed in the distance by forested areas on both sides (oaks, holly, hickory, and other species), and on the water, you will see a natural break in the spatterdock and pickerelweed vegetation. In a few hundred yards, you will reach the narrower portion of the creek where, in addition to the birds mentioned previously, you are likely to observe kingfishers, swallows, red-winged blackbirds, cormorants, a variety of ducks, and an abundance of turtles. White-tailed deer, beavers, muskrats, and fox also populate the creek and shoreline.

The creek continues to wind back and forth and is about 40 to 60 yards across here. Eventually, you will come to a fork where the main and preferred portion of the creek is to the right. In another four bends of the creek, you will come across two no trespassing signs, which marks an area of "sensitive wildlife" and is the turnaround spot. Returning to the launch site from this point is about a 3½-mile paddle, and you can also paddle up the other fork about 300 yards before having to turn around.

To extend the route, after exiting the creek, you can head right and paddle along the northern portion of Belmont Bay (toward the two tall condominium structures on the opposite side of the Occoquan River), and then up Massey Creek, described in chapter 10. Paddling up both creeks and returning to the launch site is a total of about 8 miles.

17.

Leesylvania State Park

LEESYLVANIA PARK is one of the finest parks in the Northern Virginia Regional Parks Authority, spanning 542 acres on the Potomac River between Powells and Neabsco Creeks. There is a gatehouse entry into the park that is manned during the spring through fall months. There is a $5 entry fee per car, using the honor safe when the gatehouse is unmanned. The gates are locked at 5:30 PM in the winter.

The park has five different walking trails, ranging from ⅖ mile to $2\frac{3}{10}$ miles in length, a fishing pier, a playground, and an outstanding visitors center (with restroom facilities), which includes an education center, a gift shop, and a Discovery Room housing several stuffed animals and fishes.

There are multiple put-in sites in the park, depending on whether you want a longer paddle up Neabsco Creek or a shorter paddle up Powells Creek.

Neabsco Creek

> **Directions:** Take I-95 south to exit 156, Rippon Landing. Turn left on Dale Boulevard and go to US 1 (Jefferson Davis Highway). Turn right on US 1, then left on VA 619 (Neabsco Road). In 2 miles, turn right on Daniel K. Ludwig Drive into Leesylvania State Park.
> **GPS Coordinates:** 38° 35' 16" N; 77° 15' 12" W
> **Amenities:** For Neabsco Creek, there are two main boat ramp launch sites, sign-posted as ramps 1 and 2, but these are more

for the larger power and sailboats. Farther on up the very large parking lot past boat ramp 2, at the end of the lot, is a sandy beach to launch from. Also, past boat ramp 2, at the end of the road is access to the park fishing pier, and next to the pier is the best place to launch to have the quickest access to Neabsco Creek and avoid other boating traffic, which can be quite heavy in the spring and summer months. However, you will have to portage your kayaks about 40 yards to this launch site.

Length of Paddle: 4¼–6½ miles; 2–3 hours

Route Description

After launching from either Neabsco Creek launch site, head to the left (upriver) toward the very steep rock cliffs that come down to the water's edge. Rounding Freestone point, you will see a rock that is seemingly balanced just below the water level. Freestone Point got its name because of the sandstone early settlers took from the area for building their homes and businesses. The point was also the site of a Confederate force and gun emplacement during the Civil War. Slightly farther up in one of the very tall trees at the edge of the park is an eagle's nest.

Freestone Point at Leesylvania State Park

While we have not seen eagles in the nest, we have observed two of them perched in trees nearby.

You are entering the mouth of Neabsco Creek as it flows into the Potomac River, and the land to the left is all part of Leesylvania Park. Neabsco Creek has been an important trade and commerce route since the early 1700s, but today it is used primarily for recreational purposes. Continuing along the coast, in about ½ mile you will come upon six very colorful elevated houses just below the railroad tracks and adjacent to the railroad bridge that carry both CSX transport trains and Amtrak passenger trains on their north–south routes.

Passing under the railroad bridge and entering the creek proper, there are several marinas on the left, and the first of two National Wildlife Refuges (Featherstone) are on the right bank. While at mid- and high-tide conditions, there is navigable water across a broad expanse, the main channel for Neabsco Creek is along the left side, adjacent to the marinas.

About 400 yards past the last marina on the left is the start of the second wildlife refuge, the Julie W. Metz Wetlands Mitigation Bank. This refuge has 200 acres of natural wetlands with a 2-mile birding and

Railroad ridge over Neabsco Creek

wildlife trail (accessible from Neabsco Road), where you can observe a variety of birds, including great blue herons, wood ducks, mallards, sparrows, red-winged blackbirds, woodpeckers, and hawks.

For a shorter route, turn right across the open expanse (or back along the creek at low tide), toward the Featherstone National Wildlife Refuge on the right bank. Access to this 320-acre refuge is by water landing only, and here we have observed eagles, ospreys, and pileated and red-bellied woodpeckers in the trees along the shore. The refuge is also home to white-tailed deer, red fox, raccoons, and beavers. Exiting the creek back under the railroad bridge and returning to the launch site makes for about a 4½-mile paddle.

To extend the paddle, remain in the deeper-water channel until you enter Neabsco Creek proper (where the creek narrows to about 25 yards across). You can continue up the creek for another ¾ mile before having to retrace your route. Skirting the Featherstone refuge on the return trip will result in a 6½-mile paddle.

Powells Creek

Directions: Follow directions for Neabsco Creek given above.
GPS Coordinates: 38° 35' 05" N; 77° 15' 36" W
Amenities: Access to Powells Creek is from a separate boat ramp, the first you come to after entering the park. After driving under the railroad bridge, you will see a sign to the right and a gravel road leading to the car-top launch site. There is parking for about six cars near the launch site and additional parking in a lot on the main park road about 100 yards away.
Length of Paddle: 3 miles; 1½ hours

Route Description

Departing from the small floating dock, turn right and head toward the railroad bridge and small bay beyond that provides access to Powells Creek. In the spring through fall months, expect to see upward of 20 ospreys along the length of this route, with several nests constructed on top of the out-of-season duck blinds that inhabit Powells Creek. It seems rather fitting that the ospreys would overtake these structures that are used for hunting other wildfowl to bring their young into the world. While the open water of the Potomac can become a little choppy with 10 knots of wind or more, once you cross under the bridge and enter the protected bay, the water is much calmer.

As with most paddles, hugging the shoreline provides the best opportunity for viewing wildlife. The profusion of spatterdock vegetation, wild rice plants, marsh grass, and cattails that bracket the entrance to the creek are a popular location for herons, geese, terns, wood ducks, red-winged blackbirds, and other wildfowl.

While you will notice a few townhouses among the trees on the right bank, these are the only structures that will be visible along this route. Paddling past a small point on the right brings you to the entrance to Powell's Creek.

The creek is about 50 yards wide at its entrance, but quickly necks down to about 10 to 15 yards across for most of the remainder of the route. As it meanders back and forth, you will come upon a beaver

Ospreys using duck blind for a nest

Powells Creek

lodge along the left bank, and muskrat dens are visible in the wetlands as well.

The wetlands vegetation that marks the borders of the creek eventually gives way to hard, grassy banks, where a different variety of marsh vegetation from that of the wetlands is evident, including swamp iris and marsh mallows. The creek is still about 10 yards across here, and the water below is crystal clear and several feet deep.

In a few hundred yards, you will be paralleling two rows of high-voltage transmission lines before you bend left and cross under them. You can actually hear the crackling of the electricity coursing through the very thick wires. Here is where the creek becomes a little narrower, and gravel across the streambed marks the turnaround point. While it appears that the creek would end nearby, it actually continues for several more miles and drains a watershed of over 11,500 acres. Once you have retraced your route back to the protected bay, head right and skirt the far shore for additional wildlife-viewing opportunities (on our last paddle, we observed two bald eagles soaring and landing in nearby trees). Returning to the launch site from here is about a 3-mile paddle.

18.

Ni Reservoir

Directions: From I-495 (beltway), take I-95 south to exit 130, US 3 west (Germanna Highway). Continue on US 3 for 3 miles to County Road (CR) 627 (Gordon Road). Turn left on CR 627, and follow it 4 miles to the entrance to Ni Reservoir on the right.

GPS Coordinates: 38° 14' 43" N; 77° 36' 01" W

Amenities: The reservoir is open for recreational use from the first Saturday in March through Columbus Day. Both an access and a launch fee are required. If you are not a resident of Spotsylvania County, the access fee is $7 and the launch fee is $4 per boat (cash only). The recreation area has a sand and gravel boat ramp launch site for johnboats and other small watercraft (no gasoline engines allowed). The area has parking for about 10 cars with trailers and 20 other vehicles and a large grassy area with several picnic tables and restroom facilities as well. Fishing from the bank is quite popular from the boat ramp around to the end of the open grassy area. Johnboats can be rented, but there are no kayak rentals.

Length of Paddle: 4–7 miles; 1¾–3¼ hours

Route Description

While the Ni Reservoir allows fishing from both johnboats and on the banks of the reservoir, it is relatively isolated (compared to other reservoirs in the National Capital Region) and thus an ideal paddling spot.

Departing from the boat ramp, head right and paddle around the bend past the rental boats along the shore and the grassy area of the Ni

Ni Reservoir put-in site

River Park, where more often than not, there will be several people fishing for bass, crappie, sunfish, and catfish along the bank. Paddle past
the orange buoys marking the water filtration and treatment plant. The
Ni Reservoir provides drinking water for Spotsylvania County residents, and it also is used for flood control and recreation purposes. The
400-acre reservoir was completed in 1972, and it drains an area of
about 25 square miles.

You can paddle a short distance to the far eastern part of the reservoir before turning to the left and heading up the first of many inlets,
Tealwing Cove, about ½ mile long. It was in this vicinity (on the point)
that we were treated to a bald eagle and osprey flight dance. The eagle
was in a tree along the shore that apparently was part of the osprey's
territory. The osprey dive-bombed the eagle several times, forcing the
eagle out of the tree, and continued attacking it until it flew away; quite
a sight, as the eagle was twice the size of the osprey.

After exploring the cove, turn right and head toward the western
extent of the watershed. While this stretch is fairly open, in about ⅔
mile you will come to a narrow chute about 100 yards across, and the
remaining portion of the reservoir is no more than 250 yards wide.

There are a few large houses along the shoreline, but these eventually give way to uninhabited land with beautiful wild azaleas and other flowering vegetation as you continue farther up the reservoir.

In another ¾ mile, you will come to a fork in the reservoir. Heading to the left, you can paddle another ¾ mile, steadily necking down before encountering the western terminus of the reservoir, evident by the proliferation of spatterdock vegetation in the shallow water. Here, we were escorted by dragonflies, creatures that have been around for over 250 million

Bald eagle in sweet gum tree

years, and the secluded surroundings looked like they could have been from a previous century. Exploring this cut and returning to the launch site is about a 5-mile paddle.

You can also head right at this fork, where you will shortly encounter a small island. Paddling to either side, you can continue for

Dragonfly

The Virginia Birding and Wildlife Trail

The Ni River Park, which encompasses the boat landing, is part of the Virginia Birding and Wildlife Trail network, the first statewide wildlife-viewing trail program of its kind in the country. Virginia contains every bird and animal habitat that exists between Maine and Florida, and the trail, developed in 2001 by the Virginia Department of Game and Inland Fisheries, is divided into three regional trail guides consisting of 686 sites that link wildlife-viewing sites throughout the Old Dominion.

The Coastal Trail consists of 18 separate driving loops in the eastern part of the state, from Great Falls in Northern Virginia south to the Tidewater region, and includes the Eastern Shore of Virginia. The Mountain Trail has 34 routes covering the entire western half of the state, and the Piedmont Trail has 13 routes in central Virginia, from the Dan River along the southern border to near Harpers Ferry along the Potomac River to the north.

While these trails are primarily focused on celebrating and providing access to the incredible diversity of birds, amphibians, reptiles, and mammals in the state (over 800 species), they also include information on many Civil War battlefield sites, military and memorial parks, and recreational parks.

The Battle for Virginia Loop is part of the Piedmont Trail and, in addition to the Ni River Park, includes the Fredericksburg, Chancellorsville, and Spotsylvania Courthouse battlefields and the C. F. Phelps Wildlife Management Area.

Route descriptions and information on places of interest on the Birding and Wildlife Trail can be found at www.dgif.virginia.gov/vbwt.

another ½ mile to where the cut opens up to a small cove. This is the northern finger of the reservoir, and in addition to the previously mentioned raptors, you can expect to observe red-tailed and Cooper's hawks, cormorants, downy woodpeckers, great blue herons, geese, buffleheads, mallards, and turtles.

Paddling to the end of this northern finger (where the Ni River joins the reservoir and CR 612 crosses over) along this route and returning (without exploring Tealwing Cove), is about a 6-mile paddle.

19.

Potomac River:
Algonkian Regional Park

Directions: From I-495 (beltway), take US 267 (Dulles Access Road), to exit 9, VA 28 east. Continue 5 miles on US 28 to US 7 south (Harry Byrd Highway). Follow US 7 south about 1½ miles to Cascades Parkway. Turn left on Cascades Parkway, and drive 3 miles to the park entrance.

GPS Coordinates: 39° 03' 44.3" N; 77° 22' 41.7" W

Amenities: Algonkian Regional Park is open year-round. Besides having a great boat launch ramp with a large parking lot, the park offers a host of other outdoor activities, including golf, a water park, and cottages on the Potomac River for rent year-round. Launch fees for kayaks are $2 per boat. There are no facilities at the launch site, but there are restrooms at the park office (located a few hundred yards away from the golf course pro shop). Kayak rentals and kayak tours with park authorities and a staff naturalist are available as well.

There are also several hiking and nature trails in the park, including the Gabrielson Trail, part of the Potomac Heritage National Scenic Trail. This trail is a designated National Scenic Trail corridor in the northeastern United States, which connects various trails and historic sites in Washington, D.C., Virginia, Maryland, and Pennsylvania. The trail network extends 830 miles through a portion of the Rappahannock River watershed in Virginia, the Potomac River corridor, western Maryland, and the upper Ohio River watershed in Pennsylvania.

Another interesting aspect of the park is the large deer population. We have seen upward of 80 deer wandering the golf course and surrounding parkland, completely undeterred by humans in close proximity.

The park was named after one of the largest groups of related (by dialects) Native American tribes in North America. Algonkian-speaking tribes lived in North America from coastal North Carolina to Canada, and from the Eastern Seaboard to the Rocky Mountains. More than 30 different tribes of Algonquians lived in Virginia, migrating down from the colder northern climes. They included the Powhatan, the Chesapeake, the Accomac, and the Pamunkey tribes, all whose names are associated with towns, counties, and bodies of water in eastern Virginia.

The first Native Americans that the English met at Jamestown in 1607 were Algonquians, led by Powhatan, the ruler of many groups of Algonquian Indians (known as the Powhatan Confederacy), who lived along Virginia's coastline.

Length of Paddle: 5¼–7½ miles; 2½–3½ hours

Deer at Algonkian Park

Route Description

This is one of the most challenging paddles from a fitness standpoint, because the current in the Potomac River at this particular location is the strongest of all the routes in the book. While you can paddle during any part of the tidal cycle, the current will be slightly less as the tide progresses from low to high. Also, in general, the current is strongest in a river toward the middle, lessening as you approach either shoreline. Not only is it less of a strain to paddle along the shore, you will also have a better chance at observing more wildlife.

Departing the boat ramp, head to the left upriver and against the current. The smaller island directly across from the boat ramp and extending downriver is Tenfoot Island. The main island you will encounter heading upriver shortly on the right is Van Deventer Island. This island is slightly less than 2 miles long, and you will see signs posted periodically that say hunting is allowed (but no rifles or pistols). While you can paddle along either shoreline, for the first part of the paddle, it's better to stay on the island side to avoid the 12 cabins Algonkian Park rents out.

Algonkian Park launch ramp

The lone swan in the photograph here was swimming right along Van Deventer (also called Maddux) Island. We have also seen several grebes diving, red-shouldered hawks and eagles soaring overhead, kingfishers protecting their territory, and great blue herons fishing. Van Deventer Island also appears to be home to several red-headed woodpeckers with their unique trilling call. Another fun aspect of paddling along the island is cruising under the many over-

Lone swan near Van Deventer Island

hanging river birches, sugar maples, and other trees that jut out from the shoreline.

About 1 mile into your route, you will see some exposed boulders about 30 yards from the island's shore, and more often than not, there will be several cormorants lined up with their wings spread wide. This is known as sunbathing or wing drying, and you will occasionally see the same behavior in herons and some hawks. Cormorants dry their wings so they are less buoyant and able to dive deeper while fishing. It's believed that other species of birds dry their wings to thermally regulate their bodies.

You will know when you are approaching the northern tip of the island when you see the first houses on the left bank beyond the Algonkian Park cabins. If you make it this far and to the start of the cut between Van Deventer and Selden islands (the next island upriver), you have three choices. Turning around and heading back to the boat ramp would be the shortest route (about 5¼ miles). Or you can head to the right, through the cut, and circumnavigate Van Deventer Island (about 6 miles), or head to the left and up the narrow cut adjacent to Selden Island, which extends the paddle to about 7½ miles.

If you choose to paddle around the tip of the island and out into the Potomac proper, be aware of the ripples in the current near the shoreline, indicating shallow water. Stay left toward the center of the cut to avoid beaching your kayak. Also, for this particular route, the river's current is at its strongest in this narrow swath between the two islands, and it is somewhat challenging to keep your kayak pointing into the current, as you make your way around the tip of the island. It's well worth it, though, because you will be rewarded with a much more relaxing return trip down the Potomac, which is about 350 yards wide at this point. The water is very clear, and you can see down at least 3 feet to the bottom, spotting an occasional fish or turtle swimming along. Follow along the island, and then either take the first cut to the right back to the boat ramp, or continue farther along the Potomac past Tenfoot Island and then back to the boat ramp.

Maryland

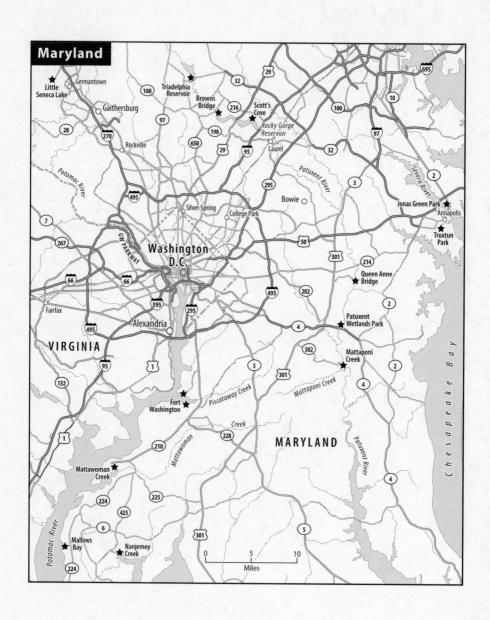

Maryland

Little Seneca Lake
Germantown
Triadelphia Reservoir
Gaithersburg
108
Browns Bridge
216
Scott's Cove
32
29
695
10
100
97
2
28
270
Rockville
97
198
650
29
95
Laurel
Rocky Gorge Reservoir
Patuxent River
Seven River
Potomac River
495
295
3
Jonas Green Park
Annapolis
7
Silver Spring
College Park
Bowie
32
Truxtun Park
267
GW PARKWAY
Washington D.C.
50
301
214
Queen Anne Bridge
66
66
202
495
2
395
295
Patuxent Wetlands Park
Fairfax
Alexandria
4
VIRGINIA
382
Mattaponi Creek
2
95
1
5
301
Mattaponi Creek
4
132
Piscataway Creek
301
Patuxent River
Fort Washington
Creek
228
MARYLAND
1
210
Mattawoman
4
Mattawoman Creek
224
225
Chesapeake Bay
6
425
301
5
Mallows Bay
Nanjemoy Creek
224

0   5   10
Miles

20.
Severn River

THE NEXT TWO routes include paddling on the historic and scenic Severn River in Annapolis, the capital of Maryland and home to the U.S. Naval Academy. The name *Severn* comes from the major river dividing England from Wales, and the archaeological evidence indicates the first humans, most likely nomadic tribes, populated its shores as far back as 5,000 to 7,000 years.

Spa Creek: Truxtun Park

Directions: From US 50, take exit 23 to MD 450; take a right on Chinquapin Road, left on Forest Drive, right on MD 665, and left on Hilltop Lane to Truxtun Park boat ramp.

GPS Coordinates: 38° 58' 07" N; 76° 29' 55" W

Amenities: Truxtun Park is one of Annapolis's largest parks, containing nature trails, a skate park, picnic tables, and two playgrounds. It also has 12 tennis courts, three baseball fields, five basketball courts, the new Roger W. Pip Moyer Recreation Center, and a large, two-ramp boat launch. The ramp is open year-round, 8 AM–5 PM, and there is a $5 launch fee per boat. Restrooms are nearby next to the tennis courts.

Length of Paddle: 4–8½ miles; 2–4 hours

Route Description

Launch to the left from the boat ramp, and taking the first cut to the left, you will come to the Silopanna Road Bridge in about ¼ mile. There will be houses and docks all along the right side, but uninhabited vegetation along the left. You can paddle another couple of hundred yards before having to turn around at the end of the cut. Reversing course and exiting this cut, continue left for another shortcut, this time with beautiful houses and boat docks on both banks. Exiting this waterway, stay left, paralleling Spayview Avenue, where you will see some of the most beautiful homes in Annapolis. You can also spot the dome and spire of the Maryland State House, designated a National Historic Landmark in 1960. It is topped by the largest wooden dome constructed without nails in the United States. Continuing past a few boating marinas, you will paddle under the Compromise Street Bridge, one of the main arteries into historic old town Annapolis. Boating traffic

Paddling toward Compromise Bridge in Annapolis

Sailboats from the Volvo Ocean Race

can often be heavy during the spring through fall months, so staying out of the main channel is recommended.

As you pass another marina on the left, you will soon encounter the vista of the grounds of the U.S. Naval Academy, founded in 1845. Again staying to the left, you will pass more sailboat marinas that mark the entrance to Annapolis Harbor and the parallel thoroughfare, Dock Street. It is at these marinas that sailors from around the world moor all sizes of sailboats, including those from the Volvo Ocean Race, the world's premier offshore sailing race.

This is a wonderful place to tie your kayak up to one of the many bollards along the rectangular basin and disembark to tour around one of the nation's most historic capital towns. It's also an ideal stopping point to enjoy the many shops and restaurants within walking distance of the harbor. Exiting the harbor, you can either retrace your route for the shortest paddle length described here (4 miles), or turn left and head out to the Severn River, passing Farragut Field where you will occasionally see midshipmen engaging in athletic events or marching drills.

The Severn River, which runs for 14 miles through Anne Arundel County, is the site of multiple college and other organizational sailing events held on a nearly year-round basis. If you happen to encounter the sailboats up close, it is important to give them right of way in accordance with the Navigation Rules of the Road.

At the point where Spa Creek joins the Severn River, turn left and head past Santee Basin, where the midshipmen dock the boats of their sailing team, and continue along past Dewey Field.

The next open body of water to the left is College Creek, and paddling up the creek, you will cross under a walking bridge and pass, on the right bank, the Naval Academy Columbarium and cemetery. You then pass under the bridges of Decatur Avenue, King George Street (MD 450), and Rowe Boulevard (MD 70). Along the left-hand side is St. John's College, a small, liberal arts college founded in 1696 as King William's School. One of the more famous aspects of the college is the annual croquet match with the U.S. Naval Academy, known as the Annapolis Cup.

The rivalry began in 1982 when the commandant of the Naval Academy told a St. John's freshman that the midshipmen could win any sports competition with the St. John's students. As the story goes, the freshman said, "What about croquet?," and when a group of midshipmen agreed to a match, the Annapolis Cup was born. Each year, the match takes place on the front lawn of St. John's College on the Naval Academy side of the campus. Music is provided by the Naval Academy band, singing by the St. John's Chorus; spectators bring blankets and picnics.

While the Naval Academy consists of a brigade of around 4,000 midshipmen, St. John's College averages about 450 students each year. The midshipmen participate in 30 varsity sports and 12 club sports, whereas St. John's has four intercollegiate teams—crew, sailing, fencing, and croquet. Even with this David versus Goliath disparity, St. John's has won the cup 25 times and the Naval Academy only 5 times!

After passing St. John's College, there is a wonderful, tranquil difference to the scenery, as the buildings and other structures give way to overhanging trees and marsh grasses along each bank. We have observed families of geese, various types of ducks, ospreys, great blue herons, cormorants, and turtles, all in this relatively short but beautiful section of the creek.

Once you reach Rowe Boulevard, you can paddle another ¼ mile up College Creek before you have to turn around. Retracing your route back to Spa Creek and Truxtun Park makes for about an 8½-mile paddle.

College Creek: Jonas Green Park

Directions: From US 50, take exit 27 (also MD 450, but not to be confused with exit 23 from the directions above) and follow it to the Naval Academy Bridge. Turn left just before the bridge on MD 648 (Baltimore Annapolis Boulevard), and take the immediate right into the entrance of the park.

GPS Coordinates: 38° 59' 43" N; 76° 29' 06" W

Amenities: This is a popular site for both launching car-top craft and fishing from the shore and the nearby concrete pier. There is ample parking, restrooms in the park headquarters building, vending machines, and no launch fee. The launch site is a sandy beach to the right of the pier and headquarters building.

Length of Paddle: 3½–7½ miles; 2–4 hours

Route Description

After launching, paddle across the Severn River and under MD 450 and the U.S. Naval Academy Bridge toward the long, concrete seawall. The water can be a little choppy during the spring through fall months, with the large amount of boating traffic including sailboat races mentioned above. The seawall adjoins Forrest Sherman field, which is another popular spot for fishing and crabbing.

Turn right up College Creek, described above, and for a short paddle (about 3½ miles), head back across the Severn toward the launch site. For a longer paddle, after exiting College Creek, you have a choice of heading into the inner Annapolis Harbor as described above (about a 6¼-mile round-trip), or heading upriver back under the Naval Academy Bridge, until you come to Weems Creek on the left (just past another small cove). Weems Creek is about 600 yards across at its mouth, necking down to about 100 yards across as you pass under the Ridgely Avenue and Rowe Boulevard Bridges. This is similar to Spa Creek in that there are houses and docks along both banks, and you can follow it about 1½ miles before having to turn around.

21.

Little Seneca Lake: Black Hill Regional Park

Directions: From I-495 (beltway), take I-270 west to exit 15A for MD 118 north (Germantown Road). Turn left onto MD 335 north (Frederick Road). Make another left onto West Old Baltimore Road. At Lake Ridge Drive, turn into the park and follow the signs to the Black Hill Regional Park Visitor Center and Boat Rental.

GPS Coordinates: 39° 11' 30" N; 77° 17' 50" W

Amenities: Black Hill Regional Park spans over 2,000 acres and includes the 500-acre Little Seneca Lake, a man-made reservoir that serves as an emergency water supply for the D.C. metropolitan area. The park is open sunrise to sunset, year-round, and you can rent kayaks, rowboats, and canoes from May through September. Each rental requires a picture ID as a security deposit. All boats must be returned by 7 PM and must have someone at least 16 years old on board. Rentals (and classes) are available as weather permits. There are restroom facilities at the visitors center, and there is a portable toilet at the boat ramp. Launch fees are $5 per kayak, payable at the boat ramp, using the honor system.

Also, there are two self-guided water trails that provide an excellent way to explore what the lake has to offer, and you can pick up laminated trail maps at the visitors center, open Mon.–Wed., noon–5 PM; Thurs., noon–2:30 PM; Sat.–Sun., 11 AM–6 PM.

Additional recreation activities in the park include miles of hiking and biking trails, lake tours, picnic shelters, volleyball courts, and a dog park. The park's staff of regional naturalists also regularly offers astronomy, kayak, and fishing programs; pontoon boat tours; and educational workshops. Other information about the park can be found at www.montgomery parks.org/facilities/regional_parks/blackhill.

Length of Paddle: 3–5½ miles; 1½–3 hours

Route Description

While Little Seneca Lake is ideal for kayaking and canoeing, it is also one of the most popular fishing destinations in the D.C. area. The lake is stocked with largemouth bass, tiger muskie, channel catfish, sunfish, and crappie, and during most times of the year, you will be jockeying with anglers launching and recovering their boats at the oversized boat ramp. The lake is plenty large enough, however, to accommodate all the watercraft on even the busiest of recreation days.

Departing from the boat ramp, head straight out toward the open part of the lake, and by staying along the right bank, you can see sev-

Water Trail marker

Graylag and Canada Geese

eral young and immature trees that are part of the Montgomery County reforestation project. The County Planning Department initiated the project in 2008 to improve water quality and wildlife habitat. You may even see a muskrat ambling among the young trees as it heads toward the brambles along the shoreline.

A little farther along, you will encounter the first of 12 water trail markers (this one happens to be number 4) that make up the Silver Thread Water Trail in this part of the lake. The second water trail covers the Little Seneca Creek Finger of the Lake and has 8 markers. Both water trails provide interesting information on the wide variety of flora and fauna you will encounter along the routes, along with some history of the area. Regarding the wildlife, several types of waterfowl make their homes here, including ospreys, eagles, graylag and Canada geese, swans, herons, and several varieties of ducks.

Probably the most prolific bird on the lake is the small and gregarious diving bird known as a coot (also known as marsh or mud hen), with their plump black bodies and white bills. We have seen flocks of over 100 quietly paddling along until you get too close to them, when

Coots in flight

many dive and those remaining take flight to escape, their wings flapping on the water sounding like a rainstorm hitting the surface.

Continuing along the right shoreline, you can explore a couple of the smaller "fingers" of this lake where water trail markers 8 through 10 describe some of the water plants, beaver activity and other types of birds you may encounter either by site or by hearing their calls. At this point, you have several options, depending on how long you want to paddle. For the shortest route, head across to the other side of the lake and toward the Little Seneca Dam, an earthen and rock fill embankment completed in 1984. Turning around here and paddling past the visitors center and adjacent sandy beach to the right and returning to the boat ramp would constitute about a 3-mile paddle. You will then be passing water trail markers 1 through 4, highlighting how the visitors center uses the lake's water to heat and cool the building, some history of the reservoir, and how cattails were harvested by the Maryland Native Americans in the past as a food source. Many animals and birds use the cattails for nesting and as cover from predators.

Second, you can continue to stay along the right shoreline, crossing under the Clarksburg Road bridge, and paddle another 1½ miles or so to the far end of the lake and the confluence of Cabin Branch Creek before turning around. Heading back to the launch ramp along this route would be about a 5½-mile paddle.

Finally, you can head across the lake, keeping the visitors center on your left, and paddle up the third major finger for the second water trail (Little Seneca Creek Finger of the Lake). At the far end of this finger is where Little Seneca Creek empties into the lake (not accessible by kayak). This water trail has eight markers, again describing some more of the history of the area, an active beaver lodge, and multiple hangouts for turtles sunning themselves. Paddling up to Little Seneca Creek and returning would be about a 5-mile paddle.

Whichever route you choose to paddle, you won't be disappointed by all that both Seneca Lake and Black Hill Regional Park have to offer. It's a destination worth visiting over and over during all seasons.

22.
Rocky Gorge Reservoir

ROCKY GORGE RESERVOIR is part of the Washington Suburban Sanitary Commission water supply distribution network, providing drinking water for Montgomery and Prince George's counties. The reservoir was constructed along the upper Patuxent, with the T. Howard Duckett Dam completed in 1952. Rocky Gorge, with 12 coves over ⅓ mile long and many shorter ones, extends over 9 miles, from the entrance of the Patuxent River in the west down to the dam in the east. With three boat ramps for access, one each to the north (Scott's Cove) and south (Sup-

Paddling past rock outcrops

plee) of the dam, and the third on the far side of the reservoir in the vicinity of the entrance of the Patuxent River (Browns Bridge), there are multiple opportunities for a variety of paddles.

The reservoir is home to a wealth of wildlife, including bald eagles, hawks, ospreys, herons, cormorants, and other diving birds, as well as beautiful wild azaleas, dogwoods, trumpet creeper (a woody vine with beautiful red blossoms), and other flowering trees and plants along the shorelines.

Boating (kayaking) is only authorized from April 1 through November 15 each year. A permit is required for all boaters and can be purchased at the Brighton Dam Road Information Center (see sidebar). For information, call 301-774-9124. Launch fees are $5 per day or $60 per year.

Scott's Cove Launch

> **Directions:** To get to Scott's Cove (number 83 on the Patuxent Water Trail) from I-495 (beltway), take I-95 toward Baltimore. Take MD 198 west (Sandy Spring Road) at exit 33. Follow MD 198 to US 29 (Columbia Pike). Go north (right) on US 29 to MD 216. Turn right onto MD 216, and go to Sweet Cherry Lane. Turn right onto Sweet Cherry Lane, and then right on Harding Road; follow the signs to the launch site.
>
> **GPS Coordinates:** 39° 08' 11" N; 76° 53' 29" W
>
> **Length of Paddle:** 3½–8¼ miles; 1½–3¾ hours
>
> **Amenities:** At Scott's Cove, there is no parking at the launch site, but there is a parking lot up on Harding Road about 50 yards away.

Route Description

Departing from the launch site, head right toward the main portion of the reservoir. Once there, you have a choice to head left toward the T. Howard Duckett Dam or right and up the longer portion of the reservoir. If there is a prevailing wind direction, it's best to head upwind first.

Brighton Dam Road Information Center

Brighton Dam Road Information Center has maps and directions for all of the put-in sites for both Rocky Gorge and Triadelphia Reservoirs (see chapter 23). Permits can be purchased online, and directions and information on all 101 sites along the Patuxent Water Trail can be found at www.patuxentwatertrail.org.

Directions: From I-495 (beltway), take exit 28, US 650 (New Hampshire Avenue) north through Colesville and Brinklow to Brighton Dam Road. After passing Brinklow, continue about 2 miles to Brighton Dam Road, turn right, and travel about 1 mile to the Brighton Dam Information Center on the right side of the road. There is a large parking area, and the information center is in the adjacent small wooden cabin. There are bathroom facilities available at Brighton Dam and portable toilets at all put-in sites.

GPS Coordinates: 39° 11' 30" N; 77° 00' 25" W

Amenities: Adjacent to the information center is a large grassy area on the other side of the dam with several picnic tables. This is a very popular spot for groups of picnickers large and small, many of which come to also visit the Washington Suburban Sanitary Commission's (WSSC) Azalea Garden Center across Brighton Dam Road. The five-acre garden center was established in 1959 and contains the largest

One word of caution: Take into consideration the prevailing wind direction and speed. Rocky Gorge reservoir is long and relatively narrow, and if the wind is at or above 10 knots (when you will just start to see whitecaps on the surface) and in a direction along the length of the reservoir, it can make for a fairly difficult paddle.

Heading toward the dam, you will curve around to the right and then have your choice of two smaller inlets on either side of the reservoir and under the Susquehanna Transmission Power lines to explore. There are then another four longer inlets, two on each side before reaching the dam about 1¾ miles from the launch site.

If you choose to head up reservoir instead, there are two inlets about the same length along the north side of the reservoir and one longer inlet a little farther up and on the left that winds back and forth

assortment of azaleas (over 20,000 blossoms) and dogwoods in the state of Maryland. The center is open daily, 8 AM–8 PM. Besides the garden center, there are also walking trails along the shoreline accessible from several of the put-in sites.

Azalea gardens at Triadelphia Landing

and contains rock outcrops that delineate the changing water levels of the reservoir.

Exploring each of these three inlets and returning to the launch site will constitute about a 5-mile paddle. To extend the route, continue up the reservoir as it bends back to the right, where you will then encounter the US 29 (Columbia Pike) bridge, one of two bridges over the reservoir (Browns Bridge being the other). Paddling to this first bridge, exploring a few of the inlets, and returning to the launch site is about a 6-mile route. To extend the route even farther, you can continue until the waterway makes a hard turn to the left and necks down to about 100 yards across, and then explore a more wide open inlet to the right, adding another 2¼ miles.

Browns Bridge

Directions: To get to Browns Bridge (number 90 on the Patuxent Water Trail) from the information center, turn right on Brighton Dam Road, go about 1½ miles, and turn right on Highland Road. Highland Road becomes US 216 (Scaggsville Road). Stay on US 216, and turn right on Browns Bridge Road. The launch ramp is about ½ mile on the left.

    Coming from Washington, D.C., and I-495 (beltway), take exit 30, US 29 north (Columbia Pike). Follow US 29 to exit 13, and turn left onto US 216 west (Scaggsville Road). In about 1 mile, make a left onto Lime Kiln Road. This is actually at a fork in the road, with the right fork continuing as US 216. Take Lime Kiln Road to the stop sign. Make a left onto Browns Bridge Road. The launch ramp is about ½ mile on the left, just over the bridge.

GPS Coordinates: 39° 08' 48" N; 76° 57' 37" W

Amenities: The boat ramp has parking for about 15 cars, and there is a portable toilet adjacent to the parking lot.

Length of Paddle: 2½–5 miles; 1¼–2½ hours

Route Description

This is a completely different paddle from the other two launch sites on this reservoir, as it is a river route instead of a more open-water route. While there is no official demarcation between the reservoir and the inflowing Patuxent River, the Browns Bridge launch site is as good a discriminator as any.

    Departing from the boat ramp, paddle under Browns Bridge and head upriver. The reservoir/river is about 45 yards wide here, but quickly begins to narrow, with stands of swamp maple trees jutting up from the water's edge on the left bank. There are several more stands of trees along either bank, and depending on the water level, there are off-shoots from the main tributary, where it's possible to paddle underneath and in between these beautiful trees. The water is relatively shallow here and very clear, making it easy to see the bottom and occasionally spot fish and rather large painted turtles under the surface.

Browns Bridge launch site

In a couple of hundred yards, the river necks down to about 30 yards across. The flat terrain on the right with a variety of trees and vegetation is part of the Patuxent River floodplain, which existed prior to the construction of the reservoir. This environment is a prime location for observing herons, geese, kingfishers, wood ducks, and red-winged blackbirds. There is also evidence of beaver activity here, with many trees neatly gnawed off at the same height. The steep banks on both sides, with occasional rock outcrops at the water's edge, make a stark contrast with the floodplain, as well as provide for a very interesting paddling route. Along with the broad diversity of

Pinxter azalea

Snowdrops

wildlife are various flowering trees and plants including pinxter azaleas and snowdrops.

A little farther up, you will come to the first of several tributaries that enter the river along the left bank, followed by rock outcrops; however, none are wide enough to explore. Just past the second tributary, the river bends to the right, and then there is a long straight stretch, nowhere more than 15 yards wide. In about ⅓ mile, you will paddle under some high-voltage transmission lines. Snell's Bridge on MD 108 (Ashton Road) is another ½ mile farther, and turning around here and returning to the boat ramp makes for a 3½-mile paddle. To extend the route, you can continue upriver about another mile, or, after returning to the boat ramp, continue down the reservoir for some open-water paddling.

23.

Triadelphia Reservoir: Greenbridge Boat Ramp

Directions: To get to the boat ramp (number 97 on the Patuxent Water Trail) from the information center, turn left onto Brighton Dam Road and continue to the stoplight at the sharp curve (about ½ mile). Turn right on Greenbridge Road. Follow this to the fishing and boating launch site.

GPS Coordinates: 39° 11' 56" N; 77° 00' 47" W

Amenities: The boat ramp is down a steep incline, and there is parking for about 30 cars.

Length of Paddle: 4½–7 miles; 2–3¼ hours

Route Description

While this description is from the Greenbridge Boat Ramp, you can also put in at the Pig Tail Area and Big Branch launch sites on the north side of the reservoir and the Triadelphia landing on the western side. All provide quick access to both the open portion of the reservoir as well as multiple narrower coves to explore.

One word of caution, take into consideration the prevailing wind direction and speed. Triadelphia Reservoir is not as long and narrow as Rocky Gorge, but a 10-knot wind (when you will just start to see whitecaps) blowing the length of the reservoir can make for a fairly difficult paddle. The wide variety of trees and other plant life makes paddling along the shore especially beautiful. There are river birches, evergreens,

Triadelphia Reservoir

Triadelphia Reservoir, like Rocky Gorge (see chapter 22), is part of the Washington Suburban Sanitary Commission water supply distribution network. The reservoir was constructed along the upper Patuxent River, with the Brighton Dam completed in 1943. Triadelphia is a little over 4 miles long and about 550 yards across at its widest point. It has multiple put-in sites and several coves and inlets to explore, with no houses or other man-made structures along their banks, and like Rocky Gorge, the reservoir has a wide variety of plants and wildlife.

Boating (kayaking) is only authorized from April 1 through November 15 each year. A permit is required for all boaters and can be purchased at the Brighton Dam Road Information Center (see sidebar in chapter 22). For information, call 301-774-9124. Launch fees are $5 per day or $60 per year.

Greenbridge launch ramp

Swamp maples at the Pig Tail put-in site

willows, sugar and swamp maples, and winterberry, among others, which are home to cardinals, woodpeckers, bobolinks, and multiple other songbirds. On the reservoir proper, you are likely to observe flocks of wood ducks and other types of ducks, ospreys, kingfishers, herons, swallows, and turtles. Motorboats are prohibited, which ensures you will have a peaceful time on the water.

For a shorter paddle, head left from the Greenbridge Boat Ramp, and after paddling along the shore for a few hundred yards and rounding the first bend to the left, head across the reservoir and up the ½-mile-long cove to the Pig Tail Area put-in site. This is marked by a

Winterberry

small boat ramp and several swamp maple trees in the water that you have to navigate around to reach the ramp site.

Other downed trees and vegetation in the water near the ramp are perfect spots for turtles sunning themselves. After turning around here, stay left and head back toward Brighton Dam. Between this cove and the next, there are areas of steep slopes and rock outcrops that extend down into the water. You will also notice evidence of a significant amount of beaver activity on this and many of the other coves extending from the main portion of the reservoir. In several locations, it appears the beavers were content with just felling the trees and leaving them in place, or sometimes just not quite finishing the job.

The next cove to the left is Nichols Cove, which you can follow for about ½ mile. After exiting this cove, you can head toward Brighton Dam, but observe the buoys across the reservoir that mark the no-boating zone in proximity to the dam. Returning to the Greenbridge Boat Ramp makes for about a 4½-mile paddle.

For a longer paddle, as you leave the boat ramp, head left away from Brighton Dam. Staying along the shore makes for both easier pad-

A beaver biting off more than he can chew

dling and more scenery to explore. You can hug the shoreline and cut in and out of several smaller coves as the reservoir begins to slightly neck down to about 200 yards across (in about 2 miles). This narrower chute continues for just short of ½ mile and leads to a fork in the reservoir. Staying left takes you up the main channel to the Triadelphia Landing area (another ¾ mile), and then the confluence of the upper Patuxent River. Taking the right fork provides another narrow cove of about ½ mile to explore. Just straight shot to the farthest cove and back is about 6 miles, and to the mouth of the Patuxent River is about 7 miles, so any additional exploring of coves would add to these distances.

24.
Patuxent River

In 1968, the State of Maryland designated the Patuxent River (the longest that flows entirely within the state) as one of its Scenic Rivers. Since then, many conservation organizations have teamed with state and local governments and volunteer groups to restore, preserve, and protect the natural resources within the watershed.

Five paddles along the river and its tributaries are given in this book, and all of them are on the Patuxent Water Trail. The water trail consists of 36 recreational and historic sites along the 110-mile length of the river, which includes 27 boat launch sites, campsites, state and national parks, and wildlife refuges. More information about the trail can be found at www.patuxentwatertrail.org.

Queen Anne Bridge Canoe Launch

Directions: From I-495 (beltway), take exit 19, US 50 east toward Annapolis. Stay on US 50 for about 7 miles, and then take exit 13, MD 301 south (Robert Crain Highway). Go 5 miles to Queen Anne Road, and turn left. Continue on Queen Anne Road for 2 1/5 miles until you see the sign for the Patuxent River 4-H Center; turn right into the center and follow the signs to the canoe launch site.

GPS Coordinates: 38° 53' 04" N; 76° 40' 33" W

Amenities: The Patuxent River 4-H (which stands for head, heart, hands, and health) Center provides teachers, students, and other organizations with a variety of hands-on activities focused on nature, agriculture, team building, leadership skills, and volunteer efforts. The center has two 40-person log cabins and an activity center and also offers a range of day and overnight camping programs.

The launch site is about ½ mile down a gravel road from the gate and consists of a very nice floating dock, a few picnic tables, and a portable toilet nearby. There is parking along the road a short distance up from the ramp. This is Patuxent Water Trail site number 52, which is about midway on the river. There is no launch fee, and in-season (May through October), you need the combination to the gate lock, which you can receive by calling 301-627-6074. Off-season, reservations are required to access the launch site and can be made by calling the same phone number.

Length of Paddle: 2–8 miles; 1½–4 hours

Route Description

Of all the routes in this book, this is the one where you will be paddling along a very narrow waterway from start to finish, no more than 20 to 30 yards across the entire route. It is somewhat shallow in certain areas, and while technically this section of the Patuxent is nontidal, the influence of tides here is minimal. You can either check the tides and paddle at or near high tide or more accurately confirm the day's water flow by going to http://md.water.usgs.gov/realtime/rt_nav/index.html. On the Web site, select the Upper Marlboro Station on the right (USGS site 01594526) and scroll down to the gauge height graph; as long as the water height is above 1½ feet, you should have no problem. (The gauge is at the MD 4 bridge, 6 miles south, but 1½ feet there translates to enough water farther upstream.) Also, the current in this part of the river is about 2 to 3 knots, and while this isn't a difficult flow to overcome, heading upriver first will ensure you are not straining at the end of the paddle to make it back to the launch site.

Departing from the launch site, head left upriver. You will soon come upon two rope swings on the left, probably used by young campers from the 4-H center. There are walking paths along both

Queen Anne Bridge launch site

banks, and many fishing spots along the left bank in the vicinity of the launch point and Queen Anne Bridge. This particular stretch of the river is marked by many submerged and partially submerged logs, with some (submerged) that extend across the entire width. However, because the water is so clear, it's not hard to pick your spots to avoid colliding with objects or beaching your kayak.

You will also come across many (mostly dry) tributaries entering from both sides of the river on this very sinewy stretch and, in the spring through fall months, several stands of elephant ear plants (also called wild taro), large, invasive plants with leaves up to 6 inches in length.

One of the more pleasant aspects of this route is the near total isolation from man-made sounds and influences. You may come across the occasional fisherman along the banks and other kayakers and canoeists, and along one small section near Queen Anne Bridge, you may hear some vehicular traffic on the nearby Patuxent River Road. Besides these minor intrusions, however, it is unlikely you will encounter any other distractions along this route.

This makes it an ideal location for observing a variety of wildlife, including spotted sandpipers flittering up- and downriver, ospreys, herons and kingfishers. Smaller hawks and kestrels, red-bellied woodpeckers, swallows, and turtles are also prevalent along the route. Around a bend to the left, you will come upon the rusted and abandoned Queen Anne Bridge, which marks the 1-mile point from the launch site. This is a convenient turnaround point for a moderate paddle, but there is navigable water for another couple of miles, upstream. Another good marking point for distance is the MD 214 (Central Avenue) bridge, 1¼ miles north of Queen Anne Bridge. This bridge, originally built in 1755 as a main connector between Anne Arundel and Prince George's counties, was replaced with the current steel truss bridge, built in the early 1900s. In the late 1940s, a heavy truck caused the bridge to buckle, and it was never rebuilt and remains in its present, unused form.

Once you have retraced your route back to the launch site, if you want to extend the paddle farther, you can continue downriver before returning back to the ramp. This stretch is a little wider and straighter, with much less debris across the width of the river. On our last paddle,

Elephant ear vegetation

Queen Anne Bridge

we encountered two paddlers who had launched at Patuxent Wetlands Park (see following route description), 6 miles downriver from Queen Anne Bridge, and were resting at the bridge put-in before making their return.

Patuxent Wetlands Park

Directions: From I-495 (beltway), take exit 11, MD 4 east (Pennsylvania Avenue), approximately 10 miles to Hills Bridge, which crosses over the Patuxent River. Take the first exit past the bridge, MD 408 (Mount Zion, Marlboro Road). At the stop sign, turn left heading over MD 4, and then take the immediate left onto Marlboro Road and follow it down to the launch site.

GPS Coordinates: 38° 48' 41"; 76° 42' 38"

Amenities: There is parking for about 8 cars adjacent to the launch site and an area farther up the road for another 10 cars. There are no restrooms at the launch site, and there is no launch fee.

Length of Paddle: 3½–7 miles; 1½–3 hours

Route Description

Patuxent Wetlands Park, number 47 on the Patuxent Water Trail, is one of the many recreational parks along the Patuxent River and arguably one of the best spots for kayaking in Anne Arundel County. Information on all of the water trail sites (27 of which are boat launch sites) along the river can be found at www.patuxentwatertrail.org.

It is important to consider the tide for this route, as it is possible to ground your kayak at lower water levels. You can either check the tides and paddle at or near high tide or more accurately confirm the day's water flow by going to http://md.water.usgs.gov/realtime/rt_nav/index .html. On the Web site, select the Upper Marlboro Station (which is at the MD 4 bridge) on the right (USGS site 01594526) and scroll down to the gauge height graph; as long as the water height is above 1½ feet, you should have no problem.

Departing from the narrow chute at the launch site, make your way out to the Patuxent River, turn right, and head away from the MD 4 bridge and the wooden fishing dock. This stretch of the river, about 40 yards across, is a very popular fishing area for both shore and boat anglers, as catfish, sunfish, rockfish, and perch travel upriver to spawn.

Wetlands

Wetlands benefit the ecosystems they occupy in several ways, and many of these are evident in the Patuxent Wetlands Park. Probably most importantly, wetlands clean (in this case) river water by filtering out sedimentation and decomposing vegetative matter, while also recycling nutrients. They prevent flooding by maintaining the river at normal water levels: during storms, wetlands absorb excess water, while during low-level periods, they slowly release water. With their large stands of emergents (plants that are firmly rooted in the bottom but extend above the surface), they can significantly slow the water flow, countering the effects of erosion. Finally, wetlands release vegetative matter into rivers, which helps feed fish and other wildlife. It's estimated that wetlands provide habitat for over one-third of the nation's threatened and endangered species.

Patuxent Wetlands Park put-in site

In a few hundred yards, you will encounter the first of the marsh grasses that make up the vast expanse of the wetlands park. Here you will find cattails, arrowhead plants, and spatterdock, along with the most important plant in the wetlands, wild rice, which provides food for hundreds of various species of birds that inhabit the park and surrounding area. There are also several birdhouses and osprey nests scattered throughout the park.

You will then pass the first of several fishing nets extending out into the river from the right bank with signs identifying the owners, and as you approach the first bend to the right, you have a choice here to head straight up one of the many interesting cuts or stay to the right to follow the river upstream. It is recommended to continue upriver, and save this first of many cuts for the return trip if you want to extend your paddle.

After the bend, along the right bank are the first of many trailers and other small structures with multiple fishing spots for the residents. These continue for a few hundred yards, and this is the only stretch of the paddle where you will encounter home sites along the river.

Farther along are several submerged sycamores with their limbs extending out of the river, and then an open expanse along the right bank with a substantial private boat dock and picnic tables. Passing the dock, there is another fork in the river with the main branch tracking off to the left. The distance to this point from the launch site is 1¼ miles. If you choose to explore the cut to the right, you will find it meanders back and forth through the marsh grasses for about 700 yards. This is one of the best areas on the route for observing wildlife. Eastern painted turtles sunning themselves, bald eagles, red-tailed hawks, ospreys soaring overhead and fishing, and skittish kingfishers and wood ducks are all likely to be observed here. All the while, you will be serenaded by cardinals, woodpeckers, red-winged blackbirds, bobolinks, and various other songbirds. On our last paddle here, we followed the circuitous cut until we came across what appeared to be the start of a beaver dam before we had to turn around.

If you decide to extend your paddle from here, after retracing your route to the river, turn right and continue upstream. This portion of the paddle is a long, fairly straight stretch with trees obscuring most of the wetlands on both sides, and it's another ¾ mile before the river

The start of a beaver dam?

necks down from 60 yards to about 30 yards across. The river continues to narrow and meander upstream from this point on, passing through several areas designated as Patuxent River Parkland, which includes another four stops along the water trail before its join-up with the Rocky Gorge Reservoir (a separate paddle in the book, see chapter 22).

You also have the option of heading back toward the launch site and paddling up the first cut mentioned previously. This cut also meanders back and forth through the wetlands, with a few more fishing nets, a couple of duck blinds, and osprey nest stands dotting the waterscape. Rounding one bend during a paddle in April, we came across a female osprey guarding her nest (probably in preparation for her young being born within the May–June time frame), while the male anxiously bleated in a nearby tree as we got closer and closer to the nest. Other wildlife you may encounter include great blue herons, egrets, bufflehead ducks, and the occasional beaver or muskrat. The total mileage for exploring the two cuts described here but not paddling farther upstream is about 4½ miles.

Osprey in nest

Mattaponi Creek: Selby's Landing

Directions: From I-495 (beltway), take exit 11A, MD 4 east (Pennsylvania Avenue). Continue about 6 miles to MD 301 south. Go 4 miles on MD 301 south, then take a left on MD 382 (Croom Road). In about 2 miles, take a left on Croom Airport Road. Follow this road until you come to a fork; take the left turn toward Selby's Landing. The road ends in the boat launch parking lot.

An alternative put-in site is Jackson's Landing at the Patuxent River Park, about 1 mile before the turn to Selby's Landing. You can paddle north upriver on this wider stretch approximately 1 mile to the entrance of Branch Creek. You can follow this narrow creek about 1½ miles before having to turn around.

GPS Coordinates: 38° 45' 09" N; 76° 59' 00" W

Amenities: Selby's Landing has parking for about 25 cars and three portable toilets at the top of the steep drive, which feeds down to the water. There is a small boat dock adjacent to the ramp and a narrow section of pebbly beach on the other side of the ramp that offers alternate launch sites from the ramp if boaters are launching or picking up their boats. Adjacent to the Jackson's Landing boat ramp, the Patuxent River Park rents kayaks and canoes.

The Patuxent River Park is part of the Jug Bay Natural Area. This 2,000-acre tract of land comprises various natural habitats that buffer the Patuxent River and provides a critical link in conserving the area's natural resources. The park has a wonderful visitors center (open daily, 8 AM–4 PM), with information about the ecology and wildlife of the Patuxent River watershed, including a live osprey cam in the spring through fall months. The park offers a wide range of outdoor recreational activities, including camping, hiking, bicycling, fishing, archaeology, and nature study. In addition, there is the Patuxent Rural Life Museums, a collection of late 19th-century and early 20th-century buildings and historic structures dedicated to preserving the rural heritage of southern Prince George's County.

Length of Paddle: 4–6½ miles; 1¾–3 hours

Jug Bay Natural Area and the Merkle Wildlife Sanctuary

Jug Bay Natural Area is part of the Chesapeake Bay National Estuarine Research Reserve in Maryland, which in turn is a nationwide network of coastal estuaries focusing on scientific research, education, and wildlife monitoring. The park is also a site on the Chesapeake Bay Gateways Network, a partnership of parks, refuges, museums, historical communities, and trails where visitors can experience and learn about the Chesapeake Bay. There are eight color-coded trails for hikers, bicyclists, and horseback riders, which provide river and wetland views and wind in and out of forested areas (trail maps are available at the visitors center).

Just to the south of Jug Bay and Mattaponi Creek is the Merkle Wildlife Sanctuary, the only one operated by the Maryland Department of Natural Resources. The sanctuary is named after Edgar Merkle, a conservationist dedicated to reintroducing Canada geese to the western shores of Maryland. Beginning with just a few breeding pairs in 1932, the sanctuary is now home to thousands of geese wintering over each year from colder climes. There is a visitors center (open weekends, 10 AM–4 PM), which has beautiful two-story views of the surrounding wetlands, fields, and ponds and highlights the life history and management of the Canada goose. In addition to the large population of geese (about 100 stay year-round), the sanctuary is also home to white-tailed deer, red fox, and nearly 200 species of recorded birds.

There are four hiking trails (open only to walkers), also color coded, ranging from ¾ mile up to 3 miles, as well as a 4-mile self-guided Chesapeake Bay Critical Area Driving Tour. This tour connects the Patuxent River Park to the north with the Merkle Wildlife Sanctuary to the south and is open for driving on Sundays only, but accessible by foot or bicycle at all times. The road winds around the historic Croom Airport and Columbia Air Center (established in 1941, it was the first African American airfield in the country) and features educational displays, observation towers, and scenic overlooks of this beautiful and unique estuarine region.

Route Description

This paddle is best done at or near high tide because, while Mattaponi Creek is a fairly wide tributary near its mouth, it contains very shallow sections throughout its length.

Leaving the boat ramp, head right downriver toward the creek. The Patuxent River is fairly wide here (about 120 yards across), but by staying along the right shore, you will come to the entrance of Mattaponi Creek in about ⅓ mile, marked by a solitary birdhouse (the first of many along the creek) on a piling in the middle of the entrance. Turn right up the creek, which is about 90 yards wide at the mouth and marked by spatterdock vegetation, marsh grass, and cattails on both banks.

When we made this paddle one February, around the first bend in the creek we came upon a large flock of common mergansers. These mergansers are relatively large diving ducks with long, slim necks, white bodies, dark heads, and orange bills.

Selby's Landing launch site

The creek quickly turns back on itself in a large bend to the right; at about this point, you will encounter the first of many beaver lodges (larger mounds made of tree branches, sticks, and dried mud) and muskrat dens (smaller mounds made of mostly marsh reeds) in various stages of repair. Paddling farther along, on the right bank is an opening that is actually a shortcut up the creek (with another beaver lodge marking the entrance), and depending on your timetable, you can take the shortcut or continue on straight up the creek proper.

The creek begins to narrow down at this point, and the variety of wildlife increases here: we have seen kingfishers, pied-billed grebes, several species of ducks, and a red-tailed hawk, screeching as it flew from tree to tree. Soon, the marsh grass gives way to trees along the left bank and eventually the right bank, and along with bald eagles and other birds of prey alighting in and out of the trees, we have observed and heard pileated woodpeckers (the largest in North America), either making their homes or sharpening their beaks.

Paddling past a beaver lodge

Critical Area Tour bridge

The creek continues to narrow, and you will paddle under a 1,000-foot-long wooden bridge that is part of the Chesapeake Bay Critical Area Driving Tour (described in the sidebar on Jug Bay Natural Area and the Merkle Wildlife Sanctuary). On our most recent paddle, we also drove this tour and saw rabbits, groundhogs, and, out in the Patuxent River, ospreys tending their young in a nest on one of the man-made osprey nest platforms.

You can continue approximately another ¼ mile before having to turn around; returning to the launch site would be about a 4-mile paddle. To extend your route, after exiting Mattaponi Creek, continue downriver and cross over to the other bank, and you will shortly come upon Lyon's Creek. This creek is about 20 to 30 yards across, and you can follow it for about 1¼ miles.

Mattawoman Creek

Directions: Take I-495 (beltway) to MD 210 (Indian Head Highway), about 1 mile from Woodrow Wilson Bridge. Continue on MD 210 for approximately 21 miles into the town of Indian

Head. Turn left onto Mattingly Avenue; follow to the end of the
road to the boat ramp.

GPS Coordinates: 38° 35' 25" N; 77° 09' 39" W

Amenities: There is parking for about 12 cars in the boat landing
area, with overflow parking and restrooms just up the road.
There are portable toilets on the edge of the parking lot. The
small white structure adjacent to the parking lot houses Up the
Creek Rentals, where you can rent kayaks, canoes, stand-up
paddleboards, and bicycles. They are open Fri.–Sun., 10 AM–
6 PM, and at other times by reservation, by calling 301-743-
3506 or 240-299-9578 (they advertise they are only 15 minutes away). Kayak rentals are $20 for two hours, or $35 for
four hours.

Length of Paddle: 4–7 miles; 1 ½–3 ½ hours

Route Description

Departing from the boat ramp, head left up the creek. There are a few
townhouses on the left bank, but these quickly give way to a long stretch
of uninhabited waterway. Across the creek is the ubiquitous marsh grass
and spatterdock vegetation, which will be present for the majority of
the paddle.

From the satellite photo of the paddling route, Mattawoman Creek
appears to be a very sinewy, rather narrow tributary from the boat
ramp up-creek. However, at higher tides, there is a large expanse of
open water for the first 2 miles of this route. When paddling at or near
high tide, it's important to read the creek and pay attention to the shallows, which are marked by grass reeds less dense than the marsh grass
proper.

The abundance of wildlife on this creek cannot be overstated. Even
in January, we observed huge flocks of mallards, white swans, and geese,
along with many hooded mergansers, great blue herons, egrets, and a
few bald eagles. On our most recent winter paddle, we flushed over 200
mallard ducks from the marsh grass shortly after leaving the boat ramp.

In the spring through summer months, in addition to these birds,
you will no doubt encounter many ospreys. It is a true spectacle of

nature to observe an osprey in its ritual fishing routine, honed over eons of evolution. It begins with the raptor soaring effortlessly overhead in circles anywhere from 30 to 200 yards above the surface of the water searching for its prey. When it locates a prospective target, it shifts to hover mode, flapping its wings to remain in place as it tracks its prospective meal. Once the osprey decides to commit to the attack, it pulls back its wings and dives straight down toward the surface, occasionally waving off if the dynamics change. If not, the osprey hits the water surface talons first and more often than not comes away with its meal. Once its prey is firmly in its grasp, the osprey then vigorously shakes from side to side to remove excess water, reducing its overall weight and making it easier to fly. On our way up-creek, we have come across several muskrat dens on the edge of the marsh and have observed a bald eagle executing some very interesting maneuvers over the water before alighting in one of the trees along the bank.

As you make your way around the second bend from the ramp, you will come across a narrow spit in the creek followed by three small

Muskrat den

islands. While you should stay to the right of all of these outcrops to remain in the deepest part of the creek, just past the spit and before the first island is the first of two navigable inlets to the left. I recommend saving this part of the paddle for the return trip, so you can make it farther up the creek and then decide whether or not to extend your route.

Once, as we came adjacent to the third island, we flushed a bevy of over 100 white swans, the first large flock of these beautiful and graceful birds we had encountered in 8 eight years of paddling. Swans are the largest members of the duck family, and among the largest of all flying birds.

Also just past the third island and to the left is the second inlet worth exploring, but this one is not as long as the first. After passing the islands, the creek starts to narrow, and the marshy area on the left is a little more swampy in nature, the perfect environment for a beaver lodge, which we have spotted on more than one occasion here.

Just past this swampy area, you will see a few houses on the hill on the left bank and the Indian Head Rail Trail paralleling the creek here (see sidebar). The round-trip distance to here without paddling up

Swans in flight

either inlet is about 4 miles. Continuing past this point, you will paddle around two more bends, and in about ¾ mile, the creek will split into three branches. By taking the middle branch (the longest of the three), you will paddle for another ¼ mile to the MD 225 (Hawthorne Road) Bridge.

Indian Head Rail Trail

Mattingly Avenue, the road accessing the boat ramp, is also one of the end points for the Indian Head Rail Trail for bicycling, running, and walking. We have biked a portion of this trail, and it is truly one of the most beautiful and well-maintained cycling pathways near Washington, D.C.

Opened in 2009, the trail was created under the National Park Service's Federal Lands to Parks Program, which helps communities develop new parks and recreation areas by transferring surplus federal land to state and local governments.

Originally, the railroad that the trail was based on was built in 1918 as a supply route for the navy's Indian Head Powder Factory. The rail bed (and now the trail) runs for 13 miles through the Mattawoman Creek stream valley, connecting the town of Indian Head to MD 301 in the town of White Plains.

Starting out from the trailhead, you will be on a slight downhill grade for the first ¼ mile, as you cross several smaller roads in the town of Indian Head. There are houses and townhouses on both sides but these quickly give way to uninhabited forested and farmland areas intermixed with marshland and small creeks. Near mile marker 2, there is a beautiful view in two directions of Mattawoman Creek, with several benches and information markers about the wildlife in the area nearby. Along with the wildlife mentioned above, it is possible to see deer, wild turkeys, butterflies, and a variety of wildflowers along the path.

Today, the trail is part of over 20,000 miles of rail trails (and more than 9,000 miles of potential rails trails) throughout the country supported by the Rails-to-Trails Conservancy, a nonprofit organization dedicated to the creation of a nationwide network of trails.

Nanjemoy Creek: Charles County Friendship Farm Park

Directions: From I-495 (beltway), take MD 210 (Indian Head Highway) toward Indian Head. Continue on MD 210 approximately 18 miles to MD 225 east (Hawthorne Road). Turn left on MD 225; go 1½ miles and turn right on MD 224 south (Chicamuxen Road). Go 1/5 mile, and turn left on MD 425 (Mason Springs Road). Continue on MD 425 south 7 miles (it becomes Ironsides Road after the intersection with MD 6), and turn left on Friendship Landing Road. The Charles County Friendship Farm Park and boat ramp is at the end of the road.

GPS Coordinates: 38° 27' 15" N; 77° 09' 02" W

Amenities: The park contains a couple of hiking trails, each about a 2-mile loop, with one snaking through the woods and the other traversing the Nanjemoy Creek. There is parking for about 12 boats with trailers and another 10 vehicles and no restroom facilities. There is no launch fee.

Length of Paddle: 5–9 miles; 2½–4 hours

Route Description

The boat ramp is open year-round, dawn to dusk. A small fishing pier is located nearby, and a short stretch of shoreline is a free-fishing area, meaning anglers do not need to possess a fishing license. This is a popular fishing area for small boat anglers, and on our most recent paddle here in January, we encountered three boaters in the smaller of the two creeks fishing for striped bass, catfish, and perch.

After launching, turn right to head up the narrower portion of the Nanjemoy Creek. To the left of the boat ramp is the larger portion of Nanjemoy Creek, which flows into the Potomac River. The Nature Conservancy established the Nanjemoy Great Blue Heron Preserve in 1978 in the forest along Nanjemoy Creek to protect a large breeding colony (over 1,000 pairs!) of great blue herons that returns here every February to nest. However, the preserve is not open to the public and only to researchers by appointment.

Nanjemoy Creek launch site

About 80 percent of the land in the Nanjemoy watershed remains forested, and while there aren't many roads, the area is being threatened by housing-development concerns and tree-clearing operations. Right now, only 690 acres (about 8 percent) of the land is protected, and The Nature Conservancy is aggressively pursuing efforts to provide protection for an additional 900 acres within the watershed. This forested area is home to bobcats, raccoons, skunks, and squirrels, along with many species of migratory birds and over 80 different types of wildflowers.

As you progress up the creek, you will encounter marsh grass along the left bank with trees and a few farms on the hillside on the right bank. Around the first bend, the creek widens out to between 200 and 300 yards across, and there is marsh grass and, in the spring through fall months, spatterdock vegetation along both banks. One of the most interesting aspects of this paddle is the large number of bald eagles. Several times, we have seen up to four eagles soaring above us, along with others perching high above in the trees along the shoreline.

Along the left shoreline are the first of several houses and boat docks as well as the first of three man-made osprey nest structures on this paddle. While the bald eagles are year-round inhabitants of the Eastern Seaboard, ospreys are migratory, and you will only see them in the D.C. area in the spring through late summer months.

Continuing up the creek, off to the right is the first of several cuts worth exploring; however, this one is best traversed at or near high tide, when you can paddle about ¼ mile before having to turn around. Just past this cut, the creek necks down to about 75 yards across with a few more houses on the left shore, which then gives way to marsh grass on both banks.

Staying along the right bank, you may notice small mounds of grass reeds a few feet inland from the creek.

Great blue heron

These are muskrat lodges, and we have seen at least 20 of them on our way up the creek. Muskrat and beaver are the only two mammals that make their homes in the water. The beaver is the larger of the two, and as you would expect, the beaver lodge (made up of tree branches, sticks, and dried mud) is typically much bigger than the muskrat den.

Now the creek starts to meander back and forth, and you will most likely observe quite the variety of wildlife as you continue farther along. We've seen Cooper's hawks flying from tree to tree, kingfishers noisily guarding their territory, rafts of mallards on the water, and the ubiquitous great blue heron flying from one fishing spot to another.

About 2 miles from the launch site, along the left bank is a small boat ramp with a few picnic tables and chairs. Just past this point, on the left, are the last two houses you will see on this paddle. To the right, around the next bend, is a marsh flat where tens of sandpipers were well camouflaged but easily spooked as we paddled by. There are over two dozen different species of sandpipers, ranging in size from the least sandpiper (about 4 inches long) to those in the curlew family (up to 26 inches long).

The creek continues to narrow down past this point, and there is a cut to the left worth exploring past the second osprey nest stand. The third osprey nest stand is another ½ mile up the creek, and just past this are open fields on the right, which mark the 3½-mile mark and a good turnaround point for a three-hour paddle.

To extend the route, continue up the ever-narrowing creek, which is navigable for another 2 miles with a combination of marsh grass, marsh flats, and trees bordering the creek and no signs of human habitation.

Muskrat den close up

25.

Piscataway Creek/Potomac River: Fort Washington Marina

Directions: From Washington, D.C., take I-495 (beltway) to MD 210 (Indian Head Highway), about 1 mile from the Woodrow Wilson Bridge. Turn right on Fort Washington Road, left on Warburton Drive, left on King Charles Terrace, and follow to the entrance of the Fort Washington Marina.

While the marina is the preferred place to launch, there is an alternate put-in site on the southern side of Piscataway Creek. Traveling farther south on MD 210 (Indian Head Highway) from Washington, D.C., turn right on Livingston Road. Turn left on Wharf Road, and follow it to the small parking area adjacent to the creek.

GPS Coordinates: 38° 42' 08" N; 77° 01' 28" W; alternate put-in site—38° 41' 40" N; 77° 00' 49" W

Amenities: Fort Washington Marina, the larger and more accessible put-in site on the north side of the creek, consists of two concrete boat ramps plus floating docks associated with a kayak shop, Atlantic Kayak Company (see www.atlantickayak.com). Although a small kayak shop, it has everything needed for the serious paddler, including top-of-the-line paddles, skirts, and wet bags. You can also schedule tours, rentals, and lessons. There is a $5 launch fee for kayaks in season. Restroom facilities are located in the Fort Washington Marina building nearby.

One of the best-kept secrets in Prince George's County is the Proud Mary Restaurant and Bar at the Fort Washington Marina. It has a fully operational tikki bar (covered and heated in the colder months) and is a perfect place to relax and have a bite to eat after paddling. All the food is cooked to order, and their crab cakes and muffins are some of the best in the D.C. area.

The second put-in site, on the south side of Piscataway Creek, consists of a very small boat ramp, but it is quite accessible for launching kayaks. This is the closer launching point to head up the narrow portion of the creek.

Length of Paddle: 4½–6¼ miles; 2–3 hours

Route Description

There are multiple routes described here that include paddling up narrow creeks as well as into and across the Potomac River. A word of caution about paddling along this stretch of the Potomac; depending on wind conditions and time of year, the water can be fairly challenging to negotiate, with the fetch (the distance the wind blows over the water) building up waves, along with swells from boat traffic. For these reasons, the portions of the routes that include the Potomac River are recommended for more seasoned paddlers.

Departing from the marina, turn left and paddle toward the upstream portion of Piscataway Creek. If you launched from the alternate put-in site, turn to the right. Stay close to the shore to observe the myriad of birds along the shoreline, including eagles, ospreys, and great blue herons.

In the spring through fall seasons, the spatterdock vegetation (see photo) overtakes a significant portion of the entryway to the creek, but it's not too difficult to maneuver around and find the entrance to the creek. Also prevalent in the open portion of the creek in the summertime are large beds of river grass, and while you can paddle through this vegetation, it's best to avoid it where possible because it can reduce your paddling efficiency.

Once you have located the entrance (much easier in winter), you can continue up the fairly narrow creek for approximately ¾ mile. As you enter the narrow creek, you will come across many types of very interesting and beautiful vegetation, including arrowhead plants, trumpet creeper, and pickerelweed, a purple flower that is a magnet in the spring and summer for black and yellow eastern tiger swallowtail butterflies.

Kingfishers, along with the rare and elusive green herons (see photo on page 170), the much smaller and more private cousins of the great blue herons, can also be found. The closer to high tide, the farther up the creek you can paddle; on one excursion, after recent rains and at high tide, we

Spatterdock flower

Fort Washington

Fort Washington has a long and varied history, dating back to its original construction and completion in 1809 (when it was known as Fort Warburton). During the War of 1812 (1809–1815), the fort, which was the only defense for the nation's capital, was destroyed by its own U.S. troops to avoid being captured by the advancing British troops, sailing up the Potomac River.

From that ignominious beginning, the fort went through several modifications, including the mounting of the first guns in 1846, additional fortification upgrades by Union troops in the Civil War, and construction of a completely new defense system called Battery Decatur in 1896. Just before World War I, the large guns of Fort Washington were removed, and it was downgraded to a harbor defense system. After the war, the fort was home to the ceremonial unit of the Military District of Washington.

During World War II, the fort served as the site for the army's Adjutant General's School, and after the war, the Veteran's Administration hospital and other government agencies occupied space here. In 1946, the fort was turned over to the Department of the Interior, and the historic park has since been managed by the National Park Service. The grounds of the park are open 8 AM to sunset and contain a 3-mile wildlife-viewing trail and picnicking and fishing sites along the Potomac River.

were able to make it a few hundred yards past the MD 210 bridge. After exiting Piscataway Creek, paddle across the bay back past the marina on the right, until you reach the Potomac River, with Fort Washington on the right point (see sidebar).

After paddling along the Potomac River past Fort Washington, you can either turn around and return to your launch point, or continue another ½ mile to the entrance of Swan Creek on the right, another wonderful, narrow, and secluded waterway to explore.

Another option is to paddle directly across the open part of Piscataway Creek to a small island where there are usually many great blue herons, ducks, cormorants, and other birds taking advantage of the shallow waters to forage for food.

Passing the island, paddle to the far shore and turn right toward the Potomac River; one tree in particular with several dead branches on the top is a prime spot for seeing bald eagles; one morning in July, we saw a pair of eagles, and while one alighted as we got closer, the other allowed us to paddle directly underneath and observe it for several minutes.

Continue along the shore to the point where Piscataway Creek and the Potomac River meet.

For a shorter paddle, you can turn right and head across the bay to Fort Washington proper, and then back to the marina or the alternate put-in site, on the south

Pickerelweed and Trumpet Creeper vegetation

An elusive green heron

side of Piscataway Creek. For a longer paddle, head across the Potomac River toward the house on the hill, Mount Vernon, home of the country's first president, George Washington. Once on the other side, you can head right, hug the shore, and head upriver to the entrance of Little Hunting Creek paddling under the concrete and stone bridge. For the really ambitious paddler, you can paddle up the creek for up to 1 mile. A more detailed description of Little Hunting Creek can be found in chapter 9.

26.

Mallows Bay: Mallows Bay Park

Directions: Take I-495 (beltway) to MD 210 (Indian Head Highway), about 1 mile from Woodrow Wilson Bridge. Continue on
MD 210 for approximately 19 miles to MD 225. Turn left on
MD 225, and continue 2 miles to MD 224 (Chicamuxen
Road), and turn right. Follow MD 224 about 11 miles, and turn
right on Wilson Landing Road. Follow the road to the entrance
to Mallows Bay Park and the boat ramp at the end of the road.

GPS Coordinates: 38° 28' 09" N; 77° 15' 49" W

Amenities: This is a very small park that the Charles County Government opened in 2010 to provide greater recreational access
to Mallows Bay. There is ample parking and portable toilets
near the boat ramp, no launch fee, historical markers, and hiking trails around the park and along the water.

Length of Paddle: 3–7 miles; 1½–3½ hours

Route Description

This is probably the most unique paddle in the book in terms of historical significance (see sidebar), the abundance and diversity of
wildlife, and the variety of paddling regimes available. If you choose,
you can tailor a route that includes any combination of three very different water types. There are two narrow creeks to explore (one on the
north and one on the south portion of the bay), the slightly more challenging obstacle avoidance route among the numerous shipwrecks, and,
finally, the open water of the Potomac River.

The launch site consists of a small boat ramp for fishing boats and a unique, floating, car-top boat launch ramp adjacent to it. Head to the left and out into Mallows Bay away from the enclosed cove to the right (this will be saved for later in the route). This portion of the bay is relatively free of obstacles, as most of the wrecks were scuttled on the

Mallows Bay

Mallows Bay contains the wrecks of more than 150 wooden steamships constructed by the U.S. government during and after World War I. While the plans called for the building of over 430 of these vessels, because of the scarcity of steel at the time, politics, corruption, and bureaucracy, only 130 were completed (and another 260 partially built) before the end of the war. It was evident that these ships were poorly designed and constructed and leaked excessively, yet the shipbuilding program continued.

It soon became apparent, however, that the journey across the Atlantic required so much coal that the ship's cargo-carrying capacity was minimized. This, coupled with the advent of the diesel engine, made the steamships obsolete by the time the war ended in 1918. In the early 1920s, most of the fully and partially constructed vessels were brought to Mallows Bay to be sold for scrap, but the reclamation project (which consisted of towing the ships to an enclosed basin, burning the wooden portions, and recovering the metal) became so expensive that it had to be abandoned. By the 1940s, many of the hulls had been salvaged by prospectors, burned to their waterlines, or left to sink into the shallow water. In addition to these wooden World War I–era ships, historians have recently catalogued many other vessels entombed here from as far back as the Revolutionary War.

In 2002, after three decades of preservation efforts by local citizens, The Trust for Public Land, which safeguards places of historical and cultural importance, protected (from commercial development) the Mallows Bay property. In 2005, the Maryland Department of Natural Resources created the Nanjemoy Resource Management Area, which includes 500 acres around Mallows Bay. In addition to the bay, the management area contains over 1 mile of undisturbed shoreline, an extensive network of wetlands, and the nearby Purse State Park and Douglas Point Special Recreation Management Area to the south.

Mallows Bay launch site

northern side of the bay. After encircling this small cove, head toward the largest and most visible shipwreck in the middle of the bay. There are no restrictions on how close you can paddle to the wrecks, and as you make your way around to the western side of the ship (toward the Potomac), you can see some of the rusted machinery and other parts of the interior of this exposed vessel.

While several wrecks have a majority of their superstructure above the water's surface, many more can only be identified by an outline of exposed and semiexposed iron bars. It is important to exercise caution paddling among these remnants, as they could potentially damage your kayak. These man-made reefs, coupled with the recent preservation efforts by the county and state, make this one of the premier spots on the Potomac River for viewing wildlife and fishing. We have observed over 20 ospreys circling overhead and attending their nests spread among the shipwrecks, many adolescent and adult bald eagles flying from tree to tree, great blue herons, multiple fish swimming among the wrecks, turtles, and a water snake (nonpoisonous).

After paddling near the previously mentioned shipwreck (with an osprey nest on its bow), head toward the second large wreck, this one

Exposed remains of a shipwreck

completely overgrown with trees and other vegetation. From this point toward the exposed dirt cliffs along the shoreline, you can paddle among the aforementioned outlines of many of the semisubmerged wrecks. As you get closer to the cliffs, you will encounter a small, sandy beach that outlines a small cove with more vessels scuttled inside of it. What appears to be an island next to the beach is another ship-wreck. There are several other wrecks jutting out from the shoreline here, parallel to each other, with most covered in vegetation.

Returning toward the launch point, you will paddle in between a

Ospreys nesting on a shipwreck

straight line of pilings before turning to the left and entering the cove adjacent to the boat ramp. There is another wreck on the far part of the cove, and the entrance to the northern creek is just to the left.

During the spring through fall months, large stands of pickerel-weed mark the entrance to the creek. It's at this point that the creek narrows down significantly, and you can paddle around several bends before you come to the first fork in the creek, marked by the remnants of a duck blind on the point, about ⅓ mile from the creek's entrance. The water is still quite deep here, and the main channel of the creek is to the right. You can paddle another 200 yards around three more bends before having to turn around.

For a longer and more challenging paddle, you can head out to the Potomac and paddle along the coast, heading either north or south (taking the prevailing wind into account). Alternatively, there is another creek on the southern portion of Mallows Bay similar to the one described above that you can follow about ¼ mile.

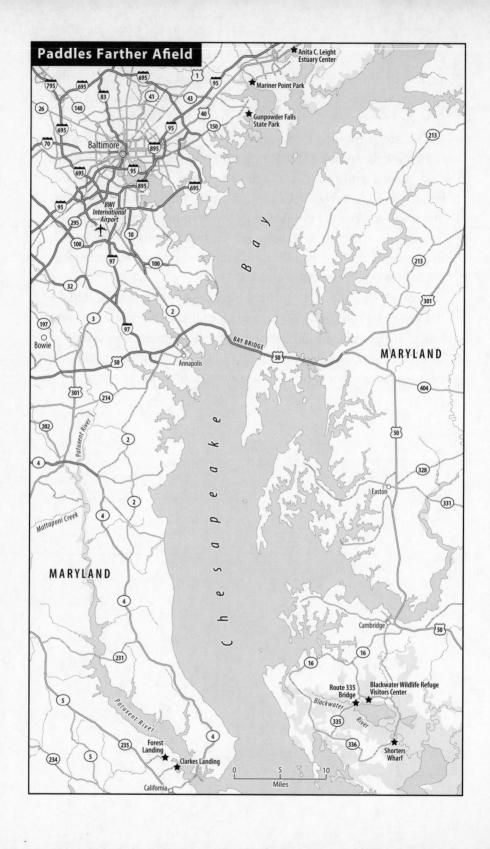

Paddles Farther Afield

Anita C. Leight Estuary Center

Mariner Point Park

Gunpowder Falls State Park

795
695
83
41
43
95
1
26
140
150
40
70
695
95
895
695
895
695
95
BWI International Airport
295
10
100
97
100
32
2
3
97
197
Bowie
50
301
214
202
2
4
2
4
Mattaponi Creek
MARYLAND
4
231
5
Patuxent River
5
235
Forest Landing
4
234
5
Clarkes Landing
California

Baltimore

Patuxent River

BAY BRIDGE
50
MARYLAND
213
213
301
404
50
328
Easton
331
Cambridge
50
16
16
Route 335 Bridge
Blackwater Wildlife Refuge Visitors Center
Blackwater
335
River
336
Shorters Wharf

B a y

C h e s a p e a k e

Annapolis

0   5   10
Miles

Paddles Farther Afield

*I*N THIS PART, I have included several routes that are just beyond an hour's drive from our nation's capital. There are two routes each to the north, east, and south of D.C., and the launch sites are all still close enough to allow for a multiple hour paddle and round-trip drive in one day. The northern and eastern routes are near small historic towns adjacent to the Chesapeake Bay (Havre de Grace and Cambridge, Maryland, respectively), and staying at a B&B or inexpensive motel makes both ideal weekend getaway locations.

The first two chapters cover three different paddling routes in one of the most beautiful and diverse areas along the Chesapeake Bay. A great starting point for getting the lay of the land is the Anita C. Leight Estuary Center, 18 miles north of Baltimore, just off US 40.

27.

Estuary Canoe Trail: Anita C. Leight Estuary Center

Directions: Take I-95 to exit 77A, US 24 south to Edgewood; turn left onto the US 40 access road. At the T, turn left onto US 40 east (Pulaski Highway). Go approximately 1½ miles, and turn right at the stoplight onto Otter Point Road. Go about ½ mile, and turn right into the driveway at the Anita C. Leight Estuary Center, 700 Otter Point Road. The launch site is at the end of Otter Point Road at the Otter Point Creek Marina, and there are no launch fees. There are restroom facilities at both the center and the marina. More information can be found at www.otterpointcreek.org.

GPS Coordinates: 39° 26' 46" N; 76° 16' 01" W

Amenities: The center provides a wealth of information about the ecology and marine biology of the Chesapeake Bay as well as launch sites and kayak routes in the region. This is one of the few remaining freshwater tidal marshes in the upper Chesapeake Bay accessible to the public. The center is open year-round: Thurs.– Sat., 10 AM–5 PM; Sun., noon–5 PM. They also offer blooming marsh kayak trips and sunset canoe trips. There are also several hiking trails in Leight Park and the nearby Melvin G. Bosley Conservancy.

Length of Paddle: 3½–7 miles; 1½–3 hours

Route Description

The Anita C. Leight Estuary Center offers a small pamphlet that describes this self-guided kayak tour through the estuary. There are several numbered markers, put in by a local Boy Scout troop (Troop 967 from Havre de Grace) that you follow around the tidal marsh. The first four markers are in the open water marking a pontoon boat pier, the eastern and western ends of Smith Park (adjacent to US 40), and an old

Havre de Grace

Havre de Grace is located on the banks of the Susquehanna River, about 10 miles north of the turn to the Anita C. Leight Estuary Center up US 40. If you have the time, it is well worth a detour to this quaint waterfront community, with a long history and maritime heritage dating back to its discovery by John Smith in 1608. The town has a wonderful mix of unique restaurants, quality bed & breakfast inns, antique and art shops, and recreational activities.

One of the little known facts about the town is that it was one of two final locations considered for our nation's capital. In 1789, when the House of Representatives voted, it was a tie, and the Speaker of the House cast the deciding vote for Washington, D.C.

Regarding the town's maritime heritage, Havre de Grace was the site of a key battle in the War of 1812. Outraged that the Americans were flying a large stars-and-stripes flag, British soldiers on 15 barges attacked the town and then burned it to the ground. The attack was a turning point in the war, as it steeled the Americans to successfully defend Baltimore. The event predated by 18 months the flying of the flag over Fort McHenry in Baltimore in September of 1814, which inspired "The Star Spangled Banner." The town holds a reenactment of the attack in May of each year.

Havre de Grace was also a key commercial port, and in 1839, the Susquehanna and Tidewater Canal was opened between the town and Wrightsville, Pennsylvania. The canal was an important transportation route of agricultural and building products for the early settlers. Use of the canal declined after the Civil War as the commercial railroad became more prevalent and cost effective. After a flood in May 1894, the canal never reopened.

piling. The fifth marker marks the entrance to the canoe trail, and the large group of trees just past the marker is called Snake Island. Eagles and ospreys can often be seen in the branches of the trees on the island.

Markers 6 through 8 direct you through the narrow waterway that is part of the 350-acre Melvin G. Bosley Conservancy, owned by the Izaak Walton League of America. It is one of the largest privately owned freshwater tidal marshes in the Chesapeake Bay watershed. At marker 9, you will come to the first lagoon, where you take a left-hand turn to stay on the trail. For a longer paddle, you can go right at the fork and continue up Winters Run for about ⅓ mile to another fork. The main creek is to the right, but you can paddle up both tributaries for about another ¼ mile before having to turn around. Exiting back to the canoe trail, turn right and you will come to signpost 10, which marks the second lagoon. When you come to marker 11, where the channel splits into three paths, stay to the left. This area is home to river otters and beavers. Lodges and other evidence of beavers are visible, such as cut-down trees and slides, where they enter and leave the water.

Signpost 14 marks the end of the narrow passageway through the conservancy, and to the right is a small lagoon where eagles and ospreys often can be seen fishing in the shallow waters. Rounding the point at signpost 15 marks the end of the kayak/canoe trail, and it is a short paddle from here back to the marina.

You can also extend this paddle by continuing along the far shore away from the marina to the next point, head across the waterway to the opposite shore, and then return to the marina.

28.

Taylor's Creek/Gunpowder Falls River: Mariner Point Park

Directions: From I-95, take exit 67A to MD 43 east (White Marsh Boulevard). Follow MD 43 to US 40 east (Pulaski Highway). Continue on US 40 east about 7 miles to Joppa Farm Road. Turn right on Joppa Farm Road, and go about 2 miles and turn right on Kearney Road. Follow the road to the entrance of Mariner Point Park. Continue past the main boat ramp to parking lot C, where the kayak and canoe launch point is on the right.

GPS Coordinates: 39° 24' 03" N; 76° 21' 04" W

Amenities: Mariner Point Park, in Harford County, is geared predominantly to water sports and fishing, although there is also a 1-mile walking trail loop that passes several gazebos on the water for picnicking and circles around a small wetlands area. There are restrooms at the park visitors center, and there is no launch fee for car-top boats.

Length of Paddle: 4–9 miles; 2–4 hours

Route Description

You will have to carry your kayak about 30 yards from the closest access point of your vehicle to the small launch point near parking lot C. Departing from the launch site, you can head either direction along Taylor's Creek. Heading right from the launch will take you up Taylor's

Creek and toward the more residential part of the route. Taking the first left, you will have the edge of the wetlands on your left and houses on the right. Even in this 50-yard-wide cut, with houses and boat docks on one side, we have observed a family of geese, ospreys, herons, terns, and swallows searching for mosquitoes and other insects. You can follow this for about ¾ mile before it dead-ends and you have to turn around.

During the summer, be prepared for *lots* of boat traffic, slowly motoring out toward Cunninghill Cove and the railroad bridge off to the left. At the park, there are over 50 parking spaces for vehicles with trailers, and on the weekends, the lots are often nearly full. Continue along this chute, with the park on the left and wetlands on the right, until you reach the open water. Stay right and skirt along the wetlands, where in the summer months, the marsh grasses can reach up to 15 feet high. Eventually, the wetlands neck down to about 30 yards across, marking the entrance to Gunpowder Falls River. You will have a very straight shot for about ¾ mile, then a big bend to the left and another

Daylilies

Puffed-up great blue heron

½-mile straight stretch before you come to the fork where the Gunpowder Falls River continues off to the left and access to a small lagoon is on the right fork.

You now have many options for continuing your route. Returning to the launch site (including the initial paddle up Taylor's Creek) is about a 5½-mile paddle (4 miles if you exclude the Taylor's Creek excursion). Paddling around the lagoon is about another mile, or you can continue up Gunpowder Falls River for about 2 miles to the Pulaski Highway Bridge, or beyond as well.

A word of caution about paddling on any of these routes; with the many narrow waterways in the wetlands and the height of the marsh grass, it's not difficult to get disoriented. It is recommended to either carry a GPS device, or be very conscious about tracking your route to make the return trip straightforward.

Another option is to return back to the point at Mariner Point Park (there is a sign on the point with a mariner statue), and paddle right around the park and up Foster Branch. There are several small islands to paddle around, and you can follow this branch for close to 1 mile.

Gunpowder Falls State Park

In addition to kayaking, this state park is a great location for a variety of other activities as well. Along with the marina for boat launching, a few yards up the road from there is Ultimate Watersports, a company that provides kayaking, stand-up paddling, windsurfing, and sailing lessons, kayak tours, and rentals. This is also the best spot for launching your kayak. The staff is extremely knowledgeable about the local surroundings and very friendly as well. More information can be found at www.ultimatewatersports.com, or call 410-335-5352.

The launch site provides direct access to Dundee and Saltpeter Creeks, as well as the Marshy Point Nature Center and Dundee Natural Environment Area. The nature center, a preserve of over 3,000 acres, has hiking trails, a canoe launch site, nature programs, and a visitors center. For more information, see www.marshypoint.org.

To get to the park, from I-95, take exit 67A to MD 43 east (White Marsh Boulevard). Follow MD 43 to US 40, and turn left on US 40 east. Go about ½ mile, and turn right at the first light onto Ebenezer Road and follow it for 4½ miles. Go past the Hammerman entrance, and enter the marina on the right. (GPS coordinates: 39° 21' 16" N; 76° 21' 31" W.)

29.

Blackwater National Wildlife Refuge

BLACKWATER NATIONAL WILDLIFE REFUGE has three marked paddling routes for kayakers and canoeists: the Orange, Green, and Purple Trails. These trails traverse the majority of the refuge and partway up the Blackwater River and Coles Creek. The distinguishing characteristic of the trails is the type of water you will be paddling in: the Orange Trail is mostly a narrow waterway that accesses Coles Creek, the Green Trail is a mix of open and more narrow water as you head up the Blackwater River, and the Purple Trail is mostly open water with a secondary spur for hardy paddlers.

One general note: It is recommended you take into account the prevailing wind direction when considering which route to paddle. This is particularly applicable to the Purple Trail because of the amount of open water on the route. A prevailing wind out of the north is preferred for all three trails as they are oriented south to north.

A very detailed, waterproof map of all three paddling trails can be purchased at the visitors center for $4. Proceeds from the sale of the map go to trail maintenance.

Directions: To get to the visitors center from I-495 (beltway), take exit 19, US 50 east, across the Bay Bridge. In about 9 miles at the US 301/US 50 split, stay right on US 50 toward Easton and Cambridge. In Cambridge, continue across the Choptank River, turn right on MD 16 west, and continue for 2 miles. Turn left on Maple Dam Road, and follow the signs to the visitors center on Key Wallace Drive.

GPS Coordinates: 38° 26' 42" N; 76° 07' 10" W

Amenities: The visitors center is the perfect place to begin your exploration of the wildlife refuge. The center is in a recently renovated two-story structure and contains a collection of wildlife exhibits, an authentic eagle's nest, an eagle and osprey cam, and a gift shop. Also around the back of the center is a butterfly and beneficial insect garden.

Visitors center hours are Mon.–Fri., 8 AM–4 PM; Sat.–Sun., 9 AM–5 PM. If you plan your trip for when the visitors center is closed, you can find additional information about paddling routes and other available activities at the U.S. Fish and Wildlife Service's Blackwater Web page at www.fws.gov/blackwater. In addition to the three marked kayak/canoe trails, which cover over 20 miles, there are four hiking trails totaling 5 miles, various cycling routes from 4 to 20 miles in length, and a 4-mile wildlife drive route.

Green Trail

Directions: Turn left out of the visitors center onto Key Wallace Drive and continue to the T at MD 335 (Golden Hill Road). Turn left on MD 335 and follow it approximately 1 mile to the launch site on the right just before the bridge.

GPS Coordinates: 38° 22' 54" N; 76° 04' 03" W

Length of Paddle: 5-8 miles; 2½-3½ hours

Amenities: The launch area for this trail is adjacent to the MD 335 bridge on Golden Hill Road and consists of a small, gently sloped sand and gravel ramp.

Route Description

The Green Trail is marked with white rectangular boxes on posts with green-colored arrows. The markers also appear on osprey nest stands, along with the letter O.

Blackwater National Wildlife Refuge

The Blackwater National Wildlife Refuge was established in 1933 by the U.S. Fish and Wildlife Service as a sanctuary for birds traveling along one of the most heavily traveled North American migration routes, the Atlantic Flyway. The flyway extends from the Canadian Maritime Provinces in the north to the Gulf of Mexico and is used by birds (as well as butterflies and some species of bats and dragonflies), primarily because there are no mountains or hills to block their flight and there are good sources of water, food, and cover over its entire extent.

The refuge's 27,000 acres, which is fed by the Blackwater and Little Blackwater Rivers, include huge areas of tidal wetlands, deciduous forests, open fields, and meadows. The name *blackwater* comes from the dark-colored waters of many rivers on the Eastern Shore, which absorb the tannins from the peat soil in the wetlands and marshes.

While the refuge is home to over 250 bird species, 35 species of reptiles and amphibians, 165 species of threatened and endangered plants, and numerous mammals, the American bald eagle is the inhabitant most people come to observe. Blackwater contains the largest breeding population of bald eagles on the Eastern Seaboard north of Florida, and many other eagles migrate to here from the colder climes of Canada and the upper northern states.

In addition to the stewardship of this unique marshland ecosystem provided by the U.S. Fish and Wildlife Service, the Friends of Blackwater, a nonprofit support group made up of volunteer citizens, organizations, and agencies, is dedicated to education about and preservation of the refuge. Information about the group and how to become a volunteer can be found at www.friendsofblackwater.org.

Departing from the ramp, head right (away from the bridge) and toward the Blackwater River to the north. Chances are very good that you will almost immediately see bald eagles (if you haven't already seen some on the drive in). On one paddle here, we observed three recently fledged eagles circling and squawking overhead, apparently just learning how to fly.

Route 335 Bridge put-in

About ¾ mile and just past the first marker (an osprey stand), you will come to a fairly wide expanse of water off to the right that marks the entrance to Buttons Creek. The creek is about 200 yards wide at its mouth and can be paddled for upward of 2 miles, although this isn't part of the Green Trail. Continuing past Buttons Creek, you will paddle around a marker at the tree-lined peninsula on the left that is an extension of Betty's Island. The next marker you will encounter is in about 1½ miles, as you make your way up Blackwater River, and the final route marker is another ½ mile beyond.

Bald eagle in flight

Paddling the Blackwater Wildlife Refuge

Purple and Orange Trails

Note that the Purple Trail is closed October 1 through March 31 to avoid interfering with migratory birds.

Directions: From the visitors center, turn right onto Key Wallace Drive. Take the right turn onto Maple Dam Road, and continue about 5¼ miles to the launch site at Shorter's Wharf.
GPS Coordinates: 38° 22' 57" N; 76° 03' 58" W
Length of Paddle: 4–11 miles; 2–5 hours
Amenities: Both trails begin at Shorter's Wharf on Maple Dam Road. There is a wide concrete boat ramp for launching and no facilities. Note that the Purple Trail can be paddled in the opposite direction if the wind is out of the south: Depart from the MD 335 bridge and turn around at Shorter's Wharf.

Route Description

The Orange Trail is marked by orange-colored arrows, while the Purple Trail is delineated by black arrows. The arrows appear on posts and on osprey nest stands. In addition to the posted markers, the Purple Trail is further distinguished by round orange buoys in the open water. Both trails share the first 1¾ miles, with the Orange Trail heading left at this point up Coles Creek and the Purple Trail heading right to the more open water.

Departing from Shorter's Wharf, head to the left and away from the bridge. In about ½ mile, you will see the first marker at a fork; stay left. In another ½ mile, you will come to the second marker, as the water opens up into a small pond. Continue north until you see the third marker, where staying to the left takes you on the Orange Trail and heading to the right keeps you on the Purple Trail.

If you choose the Orange Trail, you will be paddling up the very narrow (about 20 to 60 yards across) Coles Creek for another 2 miles to Loblolly Landing on the left bank and the final marker on this route. Returning to Shorter's Wharf is a 7½-mile paddle.

At 9 miles, the Purple Trail is the longest of the three, and it also has a 2.8-mile spur off the middle of the trail over to the entrance of the Little Blackwater River to the east. Another option, if you have the flexibility of two vehicles and you want a shorter paddle in the open water that doesn't backtrack on itself, is to launch from either Shorter's Wharf or the MD 335 bridge and recover at the other launch site.

From the fork of the Orange and Purple Trails, you will head southeast and snake around Swan and Barbadoes ponds, passing eight markers to keep you on the route before you reach the open water.

This first of several large bodies of water is Cattail Pond; head to the right where you will pick up the next marker in about 800 yards. Passing this marker, turn right and southeast toward the next two markers in close proximity, which delineate the split between the main portion of the Purple Trail to the left and up Blackwater River and the trail spur to the right, which takes you to the Little Blackwater River. Continuing on the main trail, there are an additional 10 markers, mostly on osprey stands, that guide you through several ponds, past Cole Comfort Island on the left, and then to the turnaround point at the MD 335 bridge.

30.

Patuxent River

THE TWO PADDLES described in this chapter, Forest Landing and Clarkes Landing, have many winding, narrow creeks and are close to Greenwell State Park (see sidebar), making them both enjoyable outings. The Forest and Clarkes launch areas are numbers 6 and 5 respectively on the Patuxent River Water Trail, which has over 100 different recreational sites along the beautiful and diverse Patuxent River, including 27 kayak and canoe launch sites. More information about the Patuxent Water Trail can be found in chapter 24.

Forest Landing

Directions: From I-295 (Anacostia Freeway), take exit 3A to Suitland Parkway; go 2½ miles to MD 5 (Branch Avenue). Or from the I-495 (beltway), take exit 7. Continue on MD 5 south for approximately 26 miles; take the left turn that keeps you on MD 5 south. Continue on for 8 miles until you reach MD 235 (also MD 5 for another 5 miles). Turn left on MD 235 (Three Notch Road), and go 14 miles to MD 245 (Sotterley Road). In approximately 1¾ miles, turn right on Forest Landing Road; the boat ramp and parking lot are at the end of the road.
GPS Coordinates: 38° 21' 17" N; 76° 31' 56" W
Amenities: Forest Landing has a wide boat ramp with secured piers on either side as well as a floating dock. There is ample parking, a portable toilet at the launch site, and no launch fee.
Length of Paddle: 3½–6 miles; 1½–2¾ hours

Route Description

Forest Landing is just in excess of a one-hour drive from Washington, D.C. This route consists of multiple coves and some larger creek paddling and is about 1 to 2 miles from the Patuxent River. While there are houses, boat docks, and motor- and sailboats along the majority of this route, there is still an abundance of wildlife to be found. On our most recent paddle, a great blue heron lounged along the edge of the parking lot, and as we were launching our boats, an eagle soared and circled about 50 feet above us.

Because there are smaller coves accessible on both of these routes, it is best to plan on paddling them at or near high tide to maximize your ability to navigate farther up these many narrower cuts. Departing the boat launch area, head left up the first of the two coves (Forest Landing Cove) on this route. The waterway quickly narrows, giving way to marsh grass on both sides. Eventually, you leave the houses behind and have the creek to yourselves. Depending on the tide and water level, you can paddle upward of ½ mile in the narrowing creek before you have to turn around.

Forest Landing launch site

Greenwell State Park and the Chesapeake Bay Gateways Network

Greenwell is a 600-acre state park, open sunrise to sunset, and is part of the Chesapeake Bay Gateways Network. The park offers a variety of activities, including over 10 miles of hiking and cycling trails, swimming, fishing canoeing, horseback riding, and many camping programs for children of all ages. Through the River Riders Kayaking program, the park also provides kayak outings and lessons in partnership with the College of Southern Maryland. The river riders program operates April through October.

To reach the state park, continue past Forest Landing Road on Sotterley Road until you come to Steer Horn Neck Road; turn right. Go about 1 mile to Rosedale Manor Lane on the left and the entrance to Greenwell State Park. Upon entry, a $3 donation can be made via a donation box.

The Chesapeake Bay Gateways Network is a partnership system of over 160 state and regional parks, wildlife refuges, water trails, and historic sites dedicated to helping people experience the history, natural beauty, and numerous recreational activities available throughout the entire watershed.

For more information on the network and a complete listing of all Chesapeake Bay Gateways sites, see www.baygateways.net. For those interested in volunteering, the site details the many opportunities for citizens to assist in conservation and restoration efforts of the bay's natural resources.

Passing the put-in site, the water opens up slightly as you approach Cuckold Creek (the entrance to these three coves) and Patuxent River proper. Staying along the right shore, you will come to a seawall constructed of stones, and just past the farthest point, turn right to head up the second waterway on this route. Continue about ⅔ mile until this portion begins to narrow and you encounter marsh grasses on either side of the creek.

Along both of these more isolated and interesting creeks, kingfishers can often be spotted, one of the most gregarious and territorial of waterbirds. With their distinctive shaggy crests, you will often see them

Kingfisher

flying from tree to tree with their incessant chattering, trying to avoid any contact with humans. Eventually, they will circle around back to their original tree, and you can often see the same kingfisher on your return route. We have also observed several very shy pied-billed grebes and small diving ducks. As the ducks swim, their bodies float low in the water, and when they see danger, they sink even lower and then submerge.

Retracing your route back to the launch site constitutes about a 3½-mile paddle. Once, on of our return to the launch ramp, we were serenaded by three large black dogs from one of the houses across the creek; they apparently wanted to let us know they owned the river.

To extend your route, after exiting this second cove, stay along the right shore, and you immediately come to the next cove to the south (this area is appropriately known as Three Coves). This one can be followed for about ½ mile. Finally, for some more open water paddling, you can head right after exiting the third cove into Cuckold Creek, and then left, where you will encounter a few more coves to explore.

Clarkes Landing

About 2 miles to the southeast of Forest Landing as the crow flies is Clarkes Landing. This alternate launch site offers two additional excursions worth paddling.

Directions: Same as for Forest Landing, but continue on MD 235 another 3 miles past Sotterley Road to Clarkes Landing Road: follow to the end and the boat ramp. Or turn left on Clarkes Landing Lane, and a larger parking lot and boat ramp are on the right.

GPS Coordinates: 38° 20' 32" N; 76° 30' 13" W

Amenities: Clarkes Landing consists of a gently sloping concrete ramp at the end of the lane, or you can also launch at the larger boat ramp adjacent to Clarkes Landing Restaurant (an excellent fresh seafood restaurant). There is ample parking on Clarkes Landing Lane and no launch fee.

Length of Paddle: 4–9 miles; 1¾–4 hours

Route Description

The two routes at Clarkes Landing consist of one that provides more protected water and access to a few creeks to explore and one that includes the more open water paddling in the Patuxent River, access to a greater proportion of uninhabited areas, and a few inlets as well.

If you choose to explore the creeks, head to the left, past Clarkes Landing Restaurant and up Cuckold Creek and then left again until you come to the entrance of Nat Creek. You can follow this creek about 1 mile. Exiting Nat Creek, head south and past the launch point until you come to Hickory Landing Creek on the right (passing a smaller cove to the left). This creek can be followed about ½ mile. The next creek to the south (Mill Creek) is a little wider (about 100 yards across), with significantly fewer houses along the banks, and extends for about 1 mile. Exploring these three creeks and returning to the ramp is about a 6-mile paddle.

Eroding cliffs of Myrtle Point Park

For a more isolated and open-water paddle, you can head south directly across the narrow channel to the forested point of land, part of Myrtle Point Park. The 192-acre park has several hiking trails around the perimeter with views of the Patuxent River and Mill Creek and other trails bisecting the forested inland portion.

Depending on your paddling skill and the water conditions, you can head left of the point and along the Patuxent River, where usually the water is fairly choppy from wind and boating traffic, or right into the calmer Mill Creek. Paddling along the Patuxent, you will pass the Point Patience spit on the left and the park beach on the right, and the Thomas Johnson Bridge (MD 4) is another ¾ mile.

If you retrace your route back to the point and around to the left (or if you head directly to the point), you will notice the eroding cliffs, with signs posted warning of falling trees and eroding sands. This could easily be called osprey point as well; on our last paddle, we observed upward of 30 ospreys flying, fishing, and protecting their young in nests.

Right at the closest part of the park to the launch site is the first of two small coves with very narrow entrances marked by marsh grass. Following the park around, in about 200 yards is the second enclosed feature (called Red Oak Pond), this one slightly larger. These coves offer a haven for jellyfish and other small swimmers in the warmer months because of the relatively shallower and calmer waters.

After following the perimeter of the park, you can either head across and back to the landing area or continue to the left, where you will encounter the first of three coves to explore. The first one (unnamed) is actually three small inlets; the second one, Mill Creek, extends for about 1 mile, and the third, Hickory Landing Creek, extends for about ½ mile.

Regardless of which route you choose, a visit to Clarkes Landing Restaurant after paddling is a great way to sample some wonderfully fresh seafood while enjoying the view looking out over the Patuxent River and the Thomas Johnson Bridge.

Zen and the Art of Building a Wooden Kayak

Zen, a school of Buddhism that originated in China during the sixth century, has evolved to have multiple meanings across many cultures. One definition, which I think applies to building a wooden kayak, is a total state of focus that incorporates a togetherness of body and mind.

No significant carpentry skills are required to build a kayak, nor knowledge of how boats are constructed. Once you begin the process, however, you quickly become totally immersed in the step-by-step evolution from a bunch of pieces of wood, fiberglass cloth and epoxy to something that will become a beautiful vessel to transport you across the water. I often found myself anticipating and mentally preparing for the next day's efforts.

I first became aware of the benefits of a hand-built wooden kayak in 2003, when my wife, Karen, and I first started kayaking together. We bought a 13-foot fiberglass boat for her, and I borrowed my brother Mike's wooden kayak, which he had built a few years earlier. I paddled both Karen's fiberglass kayak and my brother's wooden kayak, and there was no comparison. The wooden kayak was lighter, tracked straighter, and required much less effort to paddle.

After a couple of years of paddling his wooden kayak (a Chesapeake Light Craft, from Annapolis, Maryland), I got tired of telling everybody who asked me if I'd built it: "No, my brother did." I decided to take the plunge and attempt to build my own, and after researching the various wooden kayak Web sites and discussing it with my brother, I settled on the Pygmy series from Port Townsend, Washington (www.pygmyboats.com), mainly because I liked the lines of their boats over the other companies I looked at.

Types of Wooden Kayaks

There are two types of wooden kayak kits available, stitch-and-glue (the type I chose to construct) and strip kayaks.

Strip construction involves bending many small strips of (usually cedar) wood around temporary forms to create the kayak shape. Then, similar to stitch-and-glue kayaks, the wood is covered with fiberglass cloth and "wetted out" with epoxy to provide strength, protection, and durability.

Stitch-and-glue construction, in contrast, involves joining 6-inch-wide marine-grade plywood panels with wire twist ties, then injecting a bead of epoxy into the seams to form the shape of the kayak. Typically, stitch-and-glue kayaks, because of their wider plywood panels, are hard-chined craft, meaning they have angled edges along their keels and side panels. In contrast, strip kayaks are typically soft chined, meaning they have a rounded form for the keel and sides.

It is difficult to say which type is superior because multiple factors apply to any particular watercraft. While hard-chined designs are normally more stable craft, soft-chined kayaks are normally more efficient—but this is a generalization. It is important to do sufficient research on the trade-offs when deciding which boat you want to build. Finally, personal preference in the look and the lines of the boat can be a major factor in the overall determination.

Stitch-and-glue kits will run between $850 and $1,400, and the kits for a typical strip kayak can run $1,100 to $1,600. This may seem like an excessive amount to pay for a kayak you need to build yourself, but with minimal maintenance every few years, it will last for decades and be the envy of nearly everyone you encounter in your paddles.

Constructing a Stitch-and-Glue Kayak

The kit for a stitch-and-glue kayak comes delivered with everything you need, with the exception of a few standard tools and supplies. Included in the kit are all of the marine-grade plywood, epoxy, fiberglass cloth, wood flour (a thickening agent for the epoxy), wire, and hardware required to construct a complete kayak. You will need to have on hand an electric sander, a couple of saw horses, some wood clamps, and a few other basic tools, like wire cutters and pliers. You'll also need a box of disposable latex gloves, some small plastic cups and Popsicle sticks for mixing epoxy, and lots of quality sandpaper with varying grits.

The Pygmy Boats Web site estimates 80 to 100 hours to complete construction of a kayak, but I kept track of the first boat I built and it took about 120 hours. While this may seem like an excessive amount of time, I worked on it over the course of a winter season, and by putting in two or three hours a night, two or three nights a week, it was finished before the spring paddling season.

Working on the kayak quickly became a labor of love, and as mentioned above, I eagerly anticipated each day I worked on it. I would assiduously read the instructions, lay out the required supplies, put some music on, and dig in. There were times when I had problems and questions with a particular aspect of the instructions, and a phone call to the company quickly resolved the situation. Probably the most important aspect of building a kayak is that there is plenty of room for mistakes and deviations from a "perfect" boat. While you will notice every single flaw along the construction journey, the final product will be a beautiful boat that will provide years of paddling enjoyment.

Laying out the wood panels
IMAGE COURTESY OF PYGMY BOATS

Forming the keel
IMAGE COURTESY OF PYGMY BOATS

The stitch-and-glue construction involves joining the computer-cut panels by first drilling small holes every 6 inches along the length of the panels, inserting small pieces of wire through the holes and twisting the wire, and then running a bead of epoxy along the seams to bond the panels together. The roughed-out form of the kayak hull is established with reusable plywood forms, and once the epoxy has set (no more than 24 hours), the excess portion of the wires can be snipped off. Fiberglass cloth is then wetted down over each portion of the hull with a roller and epoxy to add durability and strength.

The most time-consuming aspect of the entire process is, by far, the sanding. Every portion of the boat requires sanding at various stages of the construction, and it is worth the extra expense, and will save you time, to purchase quality sandpaper.

After the hull dries and is sanded, the deck panels are then joined together in a single unit and, once dried, placed on top of the hull and sealed along the seams with epoxy.

The final stages involve constructing the coaming (the lip around the cockpit opening), cutting the hatch covers, applying a few coats of varnish, and installing the hardware.

Stitching the deck

"Wetting out" the deck with epoxy

Another surprising benefit of a wooden kayak is its durability. Both the kayaks I have built for our use have had significant scrapes along rocky river bottoms and concrete boat ramps. While the scrapes were noticeable, a very cursory sanding and one or two layers of varnish returned the surface to its pristine condition.

A confession: I accidentally backed into our garage door, as the door was rising up, with the kayaks on top of the car, and the aluminum door panel buckled and had to be replaced, but the kayaks were undamaged! Also, we have backed over one of the kayaks, not realizing they were on the garage floor, and while about an inch of the bow tip of one was removed, it was very straightforward to mix up some wood flour (which is part of the construction kits) with epoxy and reconstitute the bow tip. Every two to three years, sanding and varnishing the

Finished kayak

deck of the kayak—which takes only a few hours over two days to do—will make it look brand new.

So now, when we go out paddling, we are almost always met with comments like "Wow, those sure are pretty boats! Did you build them?" I can now say proudly that I did, and we invariably spend several minutes talking about both the boats and the experience of building them.

Appendix

While many of the tour descriptions in this book have associated Internet sites, listed below are several general sites that provide information on different aspects of paddling in the area.

Tides

Potomac River tides: www.saltwatertides.com/dynamic.dir/potomac sites.html

Other Virginia tributaries: www.saltwatertides.com/dynamic.dir /virginiasites.html

Maryland tides: www.saltwatertides.com/dynamic.dir/maryland sites.html

Kayak Gear and Instruction

Instructions, trips, and kayak gear: www.PotomacPaddlesports.com

Used kayaks and kayak gear: http://washingtondc.craigslist.org

Group lessons: www.potomackayaking.com

Guided tours and rentals: www.atlantickayak.com